G000144803

Collins
English
GCSE
Literature

Exam
Preparation

John Mannion

the route to Exam success for
AQA, Specification A

Published by HarpercollinsPublishers Limited
77–85 Fulham Palace Road
Hammersmith
London W6 8JB

www.**Collins**Education.com
Online support for schools and colleges

© HarpercollinsPublishers 2003

First published 2003

ISBN-13 978-0-00-710953-1
ISBN-10 0-00-710953-9

10 9 8 7 6 5

British Library Cataloguing in Publication Data

A catalogue record copy for this publication is available
from the British Library

Internal design: Ken Vail Graphic Design, Cambridge
Cover design: Barking Dog Art
Commissioning Editor: Isabelle Zahar
Project Management: Charlie Evans and Kim Richardson
Edited by Charlie Evans and Kim Richardson
Production: Katie Morris
Printed by Martins the Printers, Berwick upon Tweed

The publishers would like to thank Venessa Shakespeare for
her valuable comments on the material.

Contents

Exam Skills Focus boxes

The following topics are covered in the Exam Skills Focus boxes which occur throughout the book:

Author profile

Edward Kamau Brathwaite, one of the foremost writers and intellectuals from the Caribbean, was born in Barbados in 1930. He is both a poet and a historian; his poetry often explores the history of the development of the black population in the Caribbean. Brathwaite is also reputed to be the father of dub, which melds music and the drum beat with verse.

Limbo

And limbo stick is the silence in front of me
limbo

limbo
limbo like me
5 *limbo*
limbo like me

long dark night is the silence in front of me
limbo
limbo like me

10 stick hit sound
and the ship like it ready

stick hit sound
and the dark still steady

limbo
15 *limbo like me*

long dark deck and the water surrounding me
long dark deck and the silence is over me

limbo
limbo like me

20 stick is the whip
and the dark deck is slavery

stick is the whip
and the dark deck is slavery

limbo
25 *limbo like me*

drum stick knock
and the darkness is over me

knees spread wide
and the water is hiding me

30 *limbo*
limbo like me

knees spread wide
and the dark ground is under me

down
35 down
down

and the drummer is calling me

limbo
limbo like me

40 sun coming up
and the drummers are praising me

out of the dark
and the dumb gods are raising me

up
45 up
up

and the music is saving me

hot
slow
50 step

on the burning ground.

Edward Kamau Brathwaite

Making sense of the poem

1 **With a partner read through "Limbo" making notes on your first impressions of the poem. The following questions will focus your thoughts.**

- What does limbo mean?

- What is the purpose of the parts of the poem in italics?

- The poem mixes song and rhythm with more threatening images. Highlight those lines that seem to convey a sense of oppression or threat.

- Pull out the references to the ship and try to explain what you think is happening aboard the ship.

- What connection might there be between the beat of the drum and the limbo dance, and between the silence and the ship?

- At what point does the mood of the poem change?

- The poem tells two parallel stories. What are they and what happens in each?

- How would you explain the last four lines of the poem?

- Why do you think sounds and rhythms are so prominent in this poem?

2 **Share your understanding of the poem with the rest of the class.**

3 **In small groups prepare a reading of the poem that brings out its use of rhythm and its mood.**

BACKGROUND

Between 1450 and 1850 at least 12 million Africans were shipped as slaves across the Atlantic Ocean. The slave ships would leave from Europe for Africa, then take their "cargo" to the Caribbean (as well as other colonies in North and South America) before sailing back to Europe. The journey from Africa to the Caribbean became known as the Middle Passage.

Conditions on the ships were horrific – there was often inadequate space and food, as well as deadly diseases and mistreatment from the slave drivers. The average voyage took from five to twelve weeks and the mortality rate was high. It is said that sharks would follow the ships to feed on the disease-ravaged bodies that were thrown overboard.

The limbo dance is said to have originated on the slave ships – so the slaves could keep themselves fit and healthy when kept in cramped conditions. The dance can be seen as a metaphor for the Middle Passage – the pain and discomfort of the dancer as s/he bends backwards is likened to the horrifying journey on the ship. Once the dancer has completed the dance, however, there is a sense of jubilation. Those who survived the Middle Passage enriched the cultures they entered with new traditions and creativity.

The purpose of the poem

At first sight "Limbo" seems to be a representation on the page of a limbo dance. In this kind of dance performers take turns passing under a bar while leaning backwards. This is easy when the bar is quite high but it gets progressively more difficult when the bar is lowered. The chorus of the song that goes with the dance:

limbo,
limbo like me

is used in the poem to convey a sense of such a performance.

A closer look at the poem reveals that the descent involved in the dance is being used to remind the reader of a terrible journey on board a slave ship. This time the descent is into the darkness of the ship's hold – a descent into the darkness of horror itself. Brathwaite has used a different meaning of the word "limbo" – an unknown or intermediate place – as the starting point for this aspect of the poem. However, the ending of the dance and the end of the ship's journey are very different. The successful limbo dancer is congratulated by the crowd, whereas those who survived the sea journey from Africa to the Caribbean only had a life of slavery ahead of them.

1 Do you think using the limbo dance as a reminder of the transportation of slaves works well as an idea? Give reasons for your answer.

2 Do you think the last four lines conclude both aspects of the poem successfully?

The poet's approach

Edward Kamau Brathwaite uses language very economically in this poem. Starting with the pun on "limbo" in the title, many of the words in the poem serve two functions. The "silence in front of me" (line 1) is both the limbo stick and the long dark journey on the slave ship.

1 Copy out and fill in the table below showing other equivalents in the poem.

Object or idea	Primary meaning	Secondary meaning
Stick		whip
The dark	The night on which the dance takes place	
Long dark deck		
Darkness over me		
Dark ground		
Sun coming up		
The burning ground		

2 Sometimes the poet calls attention to the equivalents by repetition or by slight changes in phrasing. Find examples of this and comment on how they help to make the contrast between the dance and the journey.

3 In line 39 Edward Kamau Braithwaite refers to the gods as "dumb", whereas the drummers in line 41 are "praising" him. Why do you think he has made this comparison?

4 What feeling are you left with having read the poem? What do you think Brathwaite intends us to feel?

Gathering your thoughts

This poem runs two ideas together – vigorous dance and the experience of slaves on slave ships.

1 Do you think it expresses both experiences equally well?

2 Do you think it is a good idea to combine a time of torment with a kind of celebration?

3 What attitude to the past does Edward Kamau Braithwaite's poem embody?

Author profile

Tatumkhulu Afrika was born in Egypt in 1920 to an Arab father and a Turkish mother. In the 1960s he lived in Cape Town where he converted to Islam and joined the resistance to Apartheid. Arrested in 1987, he was banned from writing under his original name for five years. He therefore adopted his ANC code name as his own. "Nothing's Changed" is an autobiographical poem.

Nothing's Changed

Small round hard stones click
under my heels,
seeding grasses thrust
bearded seeds
5 into trouser cuffs, cans,
trodden on, crunch
in tall, purple-flowering
amiable weeds.

District Six.
10 No board says it is:
but my feet know,
and my hands,
and the skin about my bones,
and the soft labouring of my lungs,
15 and the hot, white, inwards turning
anger of my eyes.

Brash with glass,
name flaring like a flag,
it squats
20 in the grass and weeds,
incipient Port Jackson trees:
new, up-market, haute cuisine,
guard at the gatepost,
whites only inn.

25 No sign says it is:
but we know where we belong.

I press my nose
to the clear panes, know,
before I see them, there will be
30 crushed ice white glass,
linen falls,
the single rose.

Down the road,
working man's cafe sells
35 bunny chows.
Take it with you, eat
it at a plastic table's top,
wipe your fingers on your jeans,
spit a little on the floor:
40 it's in the bone.

I back from the glass,
boy again,
leaving a small mean O
of small, mean mouth.
45 Hands burn
for a stone, a bomb,
to shiver down the glass.
Nothing's changed.

Tatamkhulu Afrika

Making sense of the poem

This poem presents us with a picture of a person in a specific place. District Six is in Cape Town, South Africa.

1 Read the poem carefully, then draw brief sketches of the two present-day scenes described.

2 What explicit contrast between the buildings is made in the poem?

3 What contrast does the whole poem imply?

BACKGROUND

District Six used to house a large mixed-race and multi-racial community, which was popular with its residents but rather run down and generally regarded as unsafe. Jews, Muslims, blacks, whites, Indians and people of mixed ancestry lived side by side. Some claimed that District Six was the very antithesis of the government's ideology of white supremacy.

The government declared the area "whites only" and ordered the buildings to be pulled down, despite a storm of protest. District Six's 55,000 residents were forced to leave their homes, many having to relocate to the ghettos on the outskirts of the city. The outcry was so vast that the planned redevelopment of the area was never completed and remains something of a wasteland today – hence the 'amiable weeds'. The government-funded Teknicon College is the main exception.

The purpose of the poem

Tatamkhulu Afrika is very specific about his feelings in this poem. However, it would be not be a very interesting poem if the author simply said he was angry.

1 How does Tatamkhulu Afrika help us to understand and share his anger? Think about:
  • the contrast between the rich and poor in present-day District Six
  • the contrast that used to exist between black people and white people under Apartheid
  • the images used to describe his feelings.

The poet's approach

STRUCTURE

Tatamkhulu Afrika makes use of eight-line stanzas in the poem but the fourth stanza is broken up into a two-line and a six-line section.

1 Why do you think this is?

2 What do you notice about the pronouns in the two-line section?

3 How do the words in the two-line section relate to the poem as a whole?

Within the stanzas Tatamkhulu Afrika makes use of line length for emphasis. Most of the lines are multi-syllabic but two them consist of two single-syllable words. For example, "it squats" in line 19 describes the way the new hotel occupies its space. The building is clearly low and probably not very pretty but the choice of the word "squats" also implies that it shouldn't be there. These two words appearing in their own line emphasise the alien and unwelcome nature of the hotel.

4 Why do you think "Hands burn" in line 45 are given a line to themselves? How do they set up the poet's final expression of his feelings?

Tatamkhulu Afrika also makes careful use of line breaks to give prominence to important moments in his poem. Most of his lines are end stopped, each one containing a unit of grammatical sense, but occasionally he breaks this pattern, for example, when he talks about the

> ... hot, white, inwards turning
> anger of my eyes.

The short pause required before we reach the word "anger" represents a moment of suspense and emphasises his anger when it is finally mentioned.

5 **What is being emphasised by the poet detailing the different parts of his body and repeating "and the ..." in the second stanza?**

6 **Comment on the poet's use of run on lines in the following two examples:**

> ... there will be
> crushed ice white glass,
> linen falls,
> the single rose.

> Take it with you, eat
> it at a plastic table's top,

Key Terms

End stopped lines – a line is end stopped when it contains a unit of sense.

Run on lines – the sense of a run on line continues on to the next line. This causes a short pause as the eye travels back to the beginning of the next line. The ending of the line is not emphasised and rhymes, if they are present, are less noticeable. This technique is also known as **enjambment**.

LANGUAGE

1 Read the first two lines aloud. What sounds are being emphasised by the choice of words?

2 Why does the poet describe his anger as "inwards turning" in line 15?

3 Look again at the poet's description of the "whites only inn". Besides his use of the word "squats", how else does he convey his feeling that it is out of place?

4 The poem ends with the line "Nothing's changed". Reread the whole of the last stanza and then explain the power and meaning of this final line.

Gathering your thoughts

The title "Nothing's Changed" is ironic. On one level everything about District Six has changed – it has literally been wiped from the map – but at a deeper level Tatamkhulu Afrika suggests that the divisions that existed under the Apartheid regime are still very much in operation.

With a partner discuss:

1 whether you agree with Tatamkhulu Afrika's conclusion

2 if wealth always creates divisions in society

3 what particular problems occur if most of the wealth belongs to one racial group.

Grace Nichols was born in Georgetown, Guyana, in 1950. She worked as a teacher and a journalist, and spent some time in the most remote areas of the country as part of her degree at the University of Guyana. This period influenced her writing and began a strong interest in Guyanese folk tales. She came to live in Britain at the age of seventeen and now lives in Sussex with her partner, John Agard.

Deeply Caribbean in her outlook, Grace Nichols writes sensitively of other cultures and traditions, especially Africa and India.

Island Man

(for a Caribbean island man in London who still wakes up to the sound of the sea)

Morning
and island man wakes up
to the sound of blue surf
in his head
5 the steady breaking and wombing

wild seabirds
and fishermen pushing out to sea
the sun surfacing defiantly
from the east
10 of his small emerald island
he always comes back   groggily groggily

Comes back to sands
of a grey metallic soar
                    to surge of wheels
15 to dull North Circular roar

muffling muffling
his crumpled pillow waves
island man heaves himself

Another London day

Grace Nichols

Making sense of the poem

1 Approximately how long does the action of this poem take?

2 At what point would you say that the poem shifts from the Caribbean to London?

3 The emerald isle is usually a reference to Ireland. Do you think the poet is referring to Ireland here or is she making a different point?

4 Compare the adjectives used in the section of the poem about the Caribbean with those used about London. Comment on how and why they differ.

BACKGROUND

Grace Nichols has said:

"I feel at home now both in Guyana and in England. When I'm in Guyana, or another part of the Caribbean – because I see myself as coming from the wider Caribbean also – I feel I belong there because I spring from that landscape. But partly because I have children in England, I also feel at home in this culture, with their dreams and aspirations. So I embrace both. England is where I live, where I make my living, but when I'm in England I'm always looking back. Both as a writer and as an individual, I'm always looking at both worlds."

The purpose of the poem

This poem has a dedication that expresses its apparent purpose:
For a Caribbean island man in London who still wakes up to the sound of the sea

1 Do you think the poem does anything more than simply describe the process of this man waking up?

2 If you were the man mentioned in the dedication would you be pleased with the poem? Give reasons for your answer.

3 The poem presents a vision of two very different climates and societies. Do you think that Island Man would like to return to the Caribbean for good? What factors might prevent him from doing this?

The poet's approach

This poem creates two different atmospheres. At the start of the poem we have a brightly lit setting full of human and natural activity. In the second part of the poem, the human and natural elements are replaced by mechanical ones.

Grace Nichols compresses a great deal of meaning into short phrases, for instance, when she talks of "blue surf". Surf is white, so the two words evoke an image of white surf in a blue sea in the reader's mind.

1 With a partner discuss the following words and phrases and attempt to explain their full range of meanings:

- the steady breaking and wombing wild seabirds
- the sun surfacing defiantly
- ... a grey metallic roar
- surge of wheels
- crumpled pillow waves

2 Why do you think there are so many "s" sounds in the early part of the poem? Illustrate your answer with quotations.

3 Grace Nichols uses repetition and rhyme only in the middle part of the poem (lines 11–16). Why do you think she uses these linguistic effects at this point? What is happening in the poem?

Gathering your thoughts

"Island Man" is another example of someone living in two states. The man in the poem lives physically in London but his mental landscape is still dominated by images of the Caribbean.

1 Do you think that Grace Nichols feels sorry for the man in the poem? Explain your answer.

2 If you were to live away from the country where you were born or grew up for long periods, do you think you would be nostalgic for it? What things would you miss? Do you think you would remember it as it is – or just the good things about it?

Imtiaz Dharker was born in Pakistan, grew up in Glasgow and now lives in Mumbai (formerly Bombay) in India. She works as a documentary film-maker and is also an artist, conceiving her books as sequences of poems and drawings.

In an interview she describes Mumbai as "a city of grandiose dreams and structures held together with sellotape and string". "Blessing" is set in an area called Dharavi which is the largest slum in Asia. As it is not an official living area, there is often a shortage of water, made worse by the forty degree heat.

Blessing

The skin cracks like a pod.
There never is enough water.

Imagine the drip of it,
the small splash, echo
5 in a tin mug,
the voice of a kindly god.

Sometimes, the sudden rush
of fortune. The municipal pipe bursts,
silver crashes to the ground
10 and the flow has found
a roar of tongues. From the huts,
a congregation: every man woman
child for streets around
butts in, with pots,
15 brass, copper, aluminium,
plastic buckets,
frantic hands,

and naked children
screaming in the liquid sun,
20 their highlights polished to perfection,
flashing light,
as the blessing sings
over their small bones.

Imtiaz Dharker

Making sense of the poem

1 What do the first two lines tell us about the normal conditions in this place?

2 What seems to be the mood in these lines?

3 How does the poet make people think of the sound of water in the second stanza?

4 When a pipe bursts, the scene is dramatically transformed. How do adults respond to a burst water pipe?

5 How do the small children respond?

BACKGROUND

Mumbai is the third largest city in the world with a population of 18.1 million. Dharavi is a vast slum area on the outskirts of the city, a place that is home to a million people. Due to the inadequate planning for such numbers of people, there is always a shortage of clean water; the problem is made worse by the heat and sheer numbers of people who are crammed into 175 hectares of swampy, ill-serviced urban wasteland. People are drawn to Dharavi to seek employment, but many of the houses are extremely cramped and unhealthy, lacking light, ventilation and running water.

The purpose of the poem

This poem deals with water shortages in the developing world. With a partner talk about how well you think the poem works. Would it have been more effective if it had concentrated on people's suffering instead of this moment of joy?

The poet's approach

The title of the poem, "Blessing", has religious significance and the idea is picked up in the rest of the poem.

1 Copy out and fill in the table below.

Word or phrase	Religious significance
a kindly god	
congregation	
a roar of tongues	a reference to the Holy Spirit appearing at Pentecost
the blessing sings over their small bones	

2 With a partner discuss whether the poem seems to be referring to a particular religion or whether the references could be applied to several different religions.

3 The poem is very visual as well as recreating the sounds of the scene. Make a list of the words that suggest sights and sounds and which make the scene come alive for the reader.

4 How might skin crack "like a pod" (line 1)? Explain why this simile is effective.

5 With your partner discuss why Imtiaz Dharker wrote:

There never is enough water

in line 2 rather than the more usual "there is never enough water".

6 Why do you think there are so many monosyllabic words in stanza 2?

7 Explain why Imtiaz Dharker has used the word "silver" to describe the flowing water (line 9). How does this word relate to the phrase "sudden rush of fortune" (lines 7–8)?

8 Why are there no commas in the list "man woman child" in stanza 3?

9 How is the list of water-collecting items organised at the end of the third stanza?

10 Explain as fully as you can the meaning of the phrase "liquid sun" (line 19).

Gathering your thoughts

The poem describes the sudden appearance of water as if it were a religious ceremony.

1 With a partner discuss whether this approach seems effective. Does it help you to understand the importance of water in places where it is not easily available?

2 Share your ideas with the rest of the class.

3 In Britain we tend to complain about the weather and the rain. How does a reading of this poem challenge your own thinking?

Author profile

Lawrence Ferlinghetti was born in New York in 1924 and came to prominence in the 1950s as one of the "Beat" poets. The "Beat" generation was a term used to describe people who felt "beaten down" by the uncertainties of World War II and the devastation of the atomic bomb. They had to make sense of the world without relying on the certainties of previous generations.

Ferlinghetti was one of the more politically minded of the Beats and has been constantly active on the behalf of liberal causes.

Two Scavengers in a Truck, Two Beautiful People in a Mercedes

At the stoplight waiting for the light
                    nine a.m. downtown San Francisco
         a bright yellow garbage truck
                    with two garbagemen in red plastic blazers
5   standing on the back stoop
                    one on each side hanging on
         and looking down into
                    an elegant open Mercedes
         with an elegant couple in it
10 The man
         in a hip three-piece linen suit
                    with shoulder-length blond hair & sunglasses
The young blond woman so casually coifed
                    with a short skirt and colored stockings
15   on the way to his architect's office

And the two scavengers up since four a.m.
                              grungy from their route
                    on the way home
The older of the two with grey iron hair
20   and hunched back
         looking down like some
                    gargoyle Quasimodo
And the younger of the two
                    also with sunglasses & long hair
25   about the same age as the Mercedes driver

And both scavengers gazing down
                              as from a great distance
                    at the cool couple
         as if they were watching some odorless TV ad
30   in which everything is always possible

And the very red light for an instant
                    holding all four close together
         as if anything at all were possible
                              between them

35 across that small gulf
                    in the high seas
                              of this democracy

Lawrence Ferlinghetti

Making sense of the poem

This poem presents a snapshot of a scene. All the principal parts of the scene are described in order to build up a picture in the reader's mind.

1 Draw a sketch of the scene described by Lawrence Ferlinghetti. Try to include all the details mentioned in the poem, including the colours.

2 Compare your sketch with a partner's. How easy was it to construct your sketches using the details supplied by the poet?

BACKGROUND

The "American dream" is the belief that the American social, political and economic system makes success possible for every individual. In other words, the democracy of America means that freedom, equality and opportunity are available to all citizens who live there. If people work hard enough, there is nothing they cannot achieve.

Ferlinghetti's poem questions this belief by contrasting the garbagemen with the beautiful couple. It is unlikely that the garbagemen were given the opportunity to study as architects but decided to clean up rubbish instead. It will also be very difficult for them to rise very far in their profession, no matter how hard they work.

The purpose of the poem

"Two Scavengers in a Truck, Two Beautiful People in a Mercedes" works as a snapshot of a moment in Lawrence Ferlinghetti's life, but we are entitled to ask why he chose to record this particular scene. We can appreciate his intentions if we look carefully at his choice of words.

1 Why do you think he refers to the two garbagemen as "scavengers"? What level of society does this imply?

2 Who considers the people in the Mercedes to be "beautiful"?

3 What do the two young men have in common?

At the end of the poem Ferlinghetti says that the picture of the four people could be interpreted:

>   as if anything at all were possible
>   between them.

However, he describes the distance between the couples as a "small gulf" and he talks about the "high seas" of American democracy.

4 What does Ferlinghetti mean by "the high seas"?

5 What does the image of a difficult sea voyage suggest about the possibilities for these four people?

6 With a partner discuss:
   • what you understand by the American dream
   • what comment you think Ferlinghetti is making about American society by presenting this picture of people from the top and bottom of the American social scale side by side.

The poet's approach

One very noticeable characteristic of Ferlinghetti's poem is the way it looks on the page. It is not bound by formal rules of so many syllables per line or so many lines to a stanza. You could say, from this point of view, that his poetry is very informal and even democratic in its approach.

Key Terms

Line length – free verse, which does not have a regular pattern of syllables per line or lines per stanza, often makes use of line length to control the way a poem is read. Look out for very short lines, or lines which start in the middle of the page being used to emphasise particular words.

1 With a partner read the poem aloud and discuss what rule Lawrence Ferlinghetti *has* applied to his arrangement of lines on the page.

2 Ferlinghetti's choice of words is also very informal. For example, he uses a number of colloquial words and phrases, and many of his words are particularly American. Use the table below to identify and discuss the impact of these choices. Some examples have been filled in for you.

Word or phrase	British English or more formal equivalent	Effect of using this word
Stoplight	Traffic light	Helps set American context
Garbage truck		
Hip		
&		
Grungy		American slang – suggests a sort of lower class dirtiness
Odorless		

3 The poem operates by establishing the contrast between people from either end of the social spectrum. Draw up a table in which you list all of the contrasts made.

4 Which do you think are the most striking of the contrasts? Why?

The poet describes the garbage men:

> gazing down
>
>   as from a great distance
>
>   at the cool couple
>
> as if they were watching some odorless TV ad
>
>   in which everything is always possible

> And the very red light for an instant
>
>   holding all four close together
>
>   as if anything at all were possible

5 What is the effect of the phrase "as from a great distance"?

6 Three times here the poet uses the hypothetical mode "as" or "as if". What is being emphasised through this construction by the poet?

7 How would you describe the mood of the poem and your own response to the scene it presents? Refer to specific words, phrases or images to support your answer.

Gathering your thoughts

Ferlinghetti's poem is a statement about the American dream and the fact that society is not as equal as some suppose. It is undeniably true, however, that any city needs both architects and garbagemen – otherwise there would be no new buildings and filthy streets.

1 As the garbagemen perform a job that is vital to the welfare of the city and work anti-social hours to do it, is it justified that they should be paid a low wage?

2 The fact that the beautiful couple are like something out of a TV advert to the garbagemen is important. Is Ferlinghetti drawing a parallel between the reality of the American dream and the reality of the lifestyles portrayed in adverts?

Nissim Ezekiel was born in Bombay (now Mumbai) in 1924 and educated there and, later, in London. His parents were Israeli and he was brought up as an outsider to Hindu and Muslim culture. His father was a scientist; Ezekiel himself was raised as a "secular rationalist" – or atheist.

He was one of the first of the modern Indian poets to have written in English. There is a distinct personality in his poetic voice and style that reflects the modern India of urbanised western-educated Indians.

Night of the Scorpion

I remember the night my mother
was stung by a scorpion. Ten hours
of steady rain had driven him
to crawl beneath a sack of rice.
5 Parting with his poison – flash
of diabolic tail in the dark room –
he risked the rain again.
The peasants came like swarms of flies
and buzzed the name of God a hundred times
10 to paralyse the Evil One.
With candles and with lanterns
throwing giant scorpion shadows
on the mud-baked walls
they searched for him: he was not found.
15 They clicked their tongues.
With every movement that the scorpion made
his poison moved in Mother's blood, they said.
May he sit still, they said.
May the sins of your previous birth
20 be burned away tonight, they said.
May your suffering decrease
the misfortunes of your next birth, they said.
May the sum of evil
balanced in this unreal world
25 against the sum of good
become diminished by your pain.
May the poison purify your flesh
of desire, and your spirit of ambition,
they said, and they sat around
30 on the floor with my mother in the centre,
the peace of understanding on each face.
More candles, more lanterns, more neighbours,
more insects, and the endless rain.
My mother twisted through and through,
35 groaning on a mat.

My father, sceptic, rationalist,
trying every curse and blessing,
powder, mixture, herb and hybrid.
He even poured a little paraffin
40 upon the bitten toe and put a match to it.
I watched the flame feeding on my mother.
I watched the holy man perform his rites
to tame the poison with an incantation.
After twenty hours
45 it lost its sting.

My mother only said
Thank God the scorpion picked on me
And spared my children.

Nissim Ezekiel

Making sense of the poem

1 Either re-tell the story of this poem as simply as you can, or draw a cartoon strip to show the sequence of events.

2 What does Nissim Ezekiel add to his simple account to make it interesting?

3 Make a list of the things mentioned in the poem that give you a sense of place.

4 How do the neighbours respond to the situation when they cannot find the scorpion?

5 How does the father respond? How is this different from the neighbours' response?

6 How did the mother respond to her suffering?

7 What was the most remarkable aspect of the episode for the boy?

BACKGROUND

When the peasants speak of the mother's next and previous births, they are showing their Hindu beliefs. The ultimate aim of every Hindu is to obtain liberation (Moksha) which is union with God (Brahman). To achieve this a person must free themselves from the cycle of life and death. The number of times a person is reborn depends on their actions in their lifetime. These actions determine a person's karma. Positive karma enables a person to move up through the cycle towards Moksha. Negative karma moves them further down the cycle.

The purpose of the poem

This poem seems to be autobiographical – a recollection of a past event which implicitly comments on certain attitudes.

1 In small groups discuss your own childhood memories. Are early childhood memories generally pleasant or unpleasant? In what ways are your findings relevant to the poem?

2 What are the factors that have made this incident stay in Nissim Ezekiel's mind?

3 What attitudes towards his past do you think the writer expresses in this poem?

4 What do you think Nissim Ezekiel's attitude is towards each of the people who appear in the poem?

5 What further comment on people's response to suffering do you think the poet is making?

Key Terms

Autobiographical – if a poem is written in the first person it is natural to assume that the poet is speaking directly to the reader. This is not always true, however, as in some poems the writer adopts a new personality or "persona". It is a good idea to play safe with first-person poems and write "seems" to be autobiographical rather than "is".

The poet's approach

1 The scorpion makes a very brief appearance in the poem. What words are used to define its character?

2 How does Nissim Ezekiel reinforce the impression of the peasants being like flies (line 8)?

3 What does the fact that the neighbours had shadows like scorpions suggest about them?

4 How does the repetition of the phrase "they said" affect our response to the neighbours' comments?

5 Look again at lines 32–33:

> More candles, more lanterns, more neighbours,
> more insects ...

In view of his previous comments, how does this line reinforce and sum up Nissim Ezekiel's attitude to his neighbours and their actions?

6 Comment on the poet's use of alliteration and assonance in lines 34 and 35. Find other examples of alliteration in this section of the poem. Why do you think this technique is used more frequently at this point in the poem?

7 What is surprising about the father's actions in line 37? What does this show about his feelings for his wife?

8 Why do you think lines 44 and 45 are so short?

9 Why do you think that Nissim Ezekiel leaves the last words in the poem to his mother?

10 The beliefs expressed in the middle section of the poem give readers an insight into the world-view of the neighbours. Copy out and complete the following table.

Lines	What it shows
With every movement that the scorpion made his poison moved in Mother's blood ... May he sit still (16–18)	The scorpion has an almost magical effect on the mother
May the sins of your previous birth be burned away tonight (19–20)	
May your suffering decrease the misfortunes of your next birth (21–22)	
May the sum of evil balanced in this unreal world against the sum of good become diminished by your pain (23–26)	
May the poison purify your flesh of desire, and your spirit of ambition (27–28)	

11 What attitude to suffering do all these comments share?

12 Why do you think Nissim Ezekiel describes his neighbours as having "the peace of understanding" on their faces (line 31)? How does this contrast with the response of his mother and father?

Gathering your thoughts

Nissim Ezekiel records the scorpion incident with mixed feelings.

1 In small groups list the range of feelings expressed in the poem – from fear to childish wonder – and discuss which feeling, if any, seems to dominate.

2 Share your ideas with the rest of the class.

Chinua Achebe was born in Ogidi, Nigeria, the son of a teacher in a missionary school. His parents brought him up as a Christian but also installed in him many of the values of their Igbo culture.

Achebe has published many novels, poems and works of criticism. His literary language is standard English blended with pidgin Igbo vocabulary. Much of his work concerns the effects that European colonisation had on Africa.

Vultures

In the greyness
and drizzle of one despondent
dawn unstirred by harbingers
of sunbreak a vulture
5 perching high on broken
bone of a dead tree
nestled close to his
mate his smooth
bashed-in head, a pebble
10 on a stem rooted in
a dump of gross
feathers, inclined affectionately
to hers. Yesterday they picked
the eyes of a swollen
15 corpse in a water-logged
trench and ate the
things in its bowel. Full
gorged they chose their roost
keeping the hollowed remnant
20 in easy range of cold
telescopic eyes ...

     Strange
indeed how love in other
ways so particular
25 will pick a corner
in that charnel-house
tidy it and coil up there, perhaps
even fall asleep – her face
turned to the wall!
30 ... Thus the Commandant at Belsen
Camp going home for
the day with fumes of
human roast clinging
rebelliously to his hairy
35 nostrils will stop
at the wayside sweet-shop
and pick up a chocolate
for his tender offspring
waiting at home for Daddy's
40 return ...
     Praise bounteous
providence if you will
that grants even an ogre
a tiny glow-worm
45 tenderness encapsulated
in icy caverns of a cruel
heart or else despair
for in the very germ
of that kindred love is
50 lodged the perpetuity
of evil.

Chinua Achebe

Making sense of the poem

"Vultures" is divided into three sections: lines 1 to 21, lines 22 to 40 and lines 41 to 51. Each section is marked with an ellipsis (three dots) at the end. The second section has two parts, the second part starting with an ellipsis (line 30).

1 With a partner write down a short summary of each section and subsection.

You should now have a clearer idea of the logical shape of the poem. It is quite a common one, so it is worth noting. You could summarise the whole poem in this way:

Observation from life – about the vultures
Reflection on the observation – love isn't choosy about where it occurs
Further example – the Commandant at Belsen
General reflection – praise or despair.

This is quite an informal structure for a poem. It is almost like part of a conversation, which runs like this:

The other day I saw W
And that made me think of X
Which reminded me of Y
Which just goes to show Z.

2 Write your own brief conversation, filling in appropriate ideas for W, X, Y and Z.

BACKGROUND

The army seized power in Nigeria in 1966. During the civil war that followed, the Igbo people in the east of the country formed the Republic of Biafra. Chinua Achebe was in the Biafran government services and during the war he worked for the Biafran cause. By 1970 the Nigerian forces had starved the population of Biafra into submission.

The purpose of the poem

Many of Chinua Achebe's poems reflect his experiences of war. In "Vultures" Achebe conjures up a horrific image of vultures cuddling up after feeding on rotting human flesh and uses it as the basis for a reflection on how even those who seem most vicious and barbaric are capable of love towards their wives and children. His final thoughts on this matter are ambivalent and he leaves the readers to come to a conclusion for themselves.

Re-read the last section of the poem and then answer the questions.

1 In the part that runs from "Praise bounteous providence" to "cruel heart" (lines 41–47), what emotion is Achebe expressing?

2 What emotion is he expressing in the part from "or else despair" to the end (lines 47–51)? Which words or phrases suggest this emotion?

3 How would your reading of the poem have been different if these two parts had been swapped round?

4 Which of the two views expressed in this section of the poem are, in your opinion, closest to Achebe's feelings? Explain your answer.

Vultures – Chinua Achebe

The poet's approach

Achebe uses several different poetic techniques in this poem, which relate to the different sections.

"Vultures" begins as a descriptive poem.

1 Highlight the words that create a strong mood or atmosphere in the first section of the poem. What effect do they have?

2 What other poetic technique does Chinua Achebe use in the opening lines of his poem to emphasise its mood?

3 Why is the phrase "nestled close to his mate" (lines 7–8) odd in this context? What other phrase in the first section is similar in its tone?

4 What feelings are aroused by the description of the vultures and the corpse? Use quotations to support your answer.

The second section is more reflective.

5 Explain how the word "strange" (line 22) helps to change the mood of the poem at this point.

6 What poetic technique is used to describe love in this section?

7 What is a "charnel-house"? Why would you assume that love would be out of place there?

8 Achebe could have said "burned people" instead of "human roast" in line 33. Explain why this choice of words has a more powerful impact.

9 Why do you think Achebe has included the apparently minor detail of the Commandant's "hairy nostrils" (lines 34–35)?

10 Achebe follows the horrific images of the Camp and its Commandant with words that seem to give a contradictory impression of the man. Select examples of these and for each describe what image it conjures up and how this conflicts with the earlier impression.

The third section, as noted above, expresses Achebe's somewhat ambivalent conclusions.

Gathering your thoughts

In this poem Achebe is trying to makes sense of his experience of war and its horrors. He does this by reporting his observations and his thoughts about them but he does not come to a very clear conclusion.

With a partner discuss the following questions.

1 Do you agree with Achebe's approach? Will evil always be a mystery or can it be understood?

2 Would you have preferred a more definite conclusion? Or at least a clearer indication of Achebe's own feelings?

Author profile

Denise Levertov was born in Ilford, Essex, in 1923. During World War II she worked as a nurse in London throughout the bombings. She later settled in New York City and became a naturalised American citizen in 1956.

Levertov became an important and acclaimed voice in the American poetry scene. During the 1960s, feminism, activism and the Vietnam War became prominent in her poetry. She died in 1997.

What Were They Like?

1) Did the people of Viet Nam
   use lanterns of stone?
2) Did they hold ceremonies
   to reverence the opening of buds?
3) Were they inclined to quiet laughter?
4) Did they use bone and ivory,
   jade and silver, for ornament?
5) Had they an epic poem?
6) Did they distinguish between speech and singing?

1) Sir, their light hearts turned to stone.
   It is not remembered whether in gardens
   stone lanterns illumined peasant ways.
2) Perhaps they gathered once to delight in blossom,
   but after the children were killed
   there were no more buds.
3) Sir, laughter is bitter to the burned mouth.
4) A dream ago, perhaps. Ornament is for joy.
   All the bones were charred.
5) It is not remembered. Remember,
   most were peasants; their life
   was in rice and bamboo.
   When peaceful clouds were reflected in the paddies
   and the water buffalo stepped surely among terraces,
   maybe fathers told their sons old tales.
   When bombs smashed those mirrors
   there was time only to scream.
6) There is an echo yet
   of their speech which was like a song.
   It was reported that their singing resembled
   the flight of moths in moonlight.
   Who can say? It is silent now.

Denise Levertov

Making sense of the poem

1 What kind of people is the question "What were they like?" asked about? Who do you imagine to be asking the question?

2 What does the poem imply about the people of Vietnam? Refer to particular words or lines in your answers.

3 Try reading the poem out loud with a partner, taking the different parts. How should the questions be read? What tone of voice is appropriate for the person answering the questions? In the answer to questions 1 and 3, the person begins with "Sir". How do you think this word is said? Is it merely polite and formal? Might there be an underlying sense of frustration at the ignorance of the enquirer; or is a sad, reflective tone more appropriate?

BACKGROUND

The Vietnam War (1964–75) was a lengthy and unsuccessful effort by South Vietnam and the United States to prevent the communists of North Vietnam from uniting South Vietnam with North Vietnam under their leadership.

The length of the war, the high number of American casualties, and the exposure of US involvement in war crimes (such as a massacre at My Lai) helped to turn many in the United States against the war. There were huge public demonstrations in Washington, D.C., as well as in many other cities in the United States and on college campuses.

The war did not end, despite peace agreements in 1973, until North Vietnam's successful offensive in 1975. South Vietnam's request for aid was denied by the US Congress and their resistance collapsed. North Vietnamese troops marched into Saigon and the country was unified. 58,000 Americans and 216,000 Vietnamese died in the fighting.

The purpose of the poem

Denise Levertov is an American poet and this poem was written as a reflection on her country's war with Vietnam.

1 Since we know that the people of Vietnam were not actually wiped out, what does the poem suggest was actually lost in the war?

2 The poem was written in 1971, before the end of the war. How does this affect the way you read the poem?

3 Do you think Denise Levertov's approach fulfils her purpose better than, say, describing the horrors of the war in Vietnam directly? Give your reasons.

The poet's approach

STRUCTURE

"What Were They Like?" begins with six questions which are then answered.

1 What picture of the people of Vietnam is built up in the questions section?

2 What story do the answers tell about the people of Vietnam?

3 Discuss the answers to the questions with a partner. What do you understand by the answer to the first five? What do you understand from the answer to question six?

4 Decide whether you think Levertov's arrangement works better than following each question with its answer. Give your reasons.

LANGUAGE

This poem makes use of symbolism. For example, the answer to the question about the ceremonies to commemorate the opening of buds states that:

... after the children were killed
there were no more buds.

This reply does not make sense in ordinary terms – why would the death of children affect natural processes like the opening of buds? However, once we realise that the buds symbolise the children, the meaning is clear. In fact, the original ceremonies probably embraced this symbolic connection between young children and young plants. Without children the ceremonies became meaningless.

1 **Comment on Denise Levertov's use of symbolism in the following lines:**

... their light hearts turned to stone   All the bones were charred.

2 **Comment on her use of metaphor in the phrase:**

When bombs smashed those mirrors.

3 **Comment on the use of simile in:**

... their speech which was like a song   ... their singing resembled
the flight of moths in moonlight.

4 **Why are there so many comparisons in this poem?**

Key Terms

Symbolism – a form of comparison where something is used to stand for another.

Simile – a figure of speech where one thing is compared to another explicitly using "as" or "like".

Metaphor – a figure of speech where it is stated that one thing is another.

Gathering your thoughts

Denise Levertov's poem is an attempt to express a sense of loss. The positive things she mentions in the poem are almost all delicate or fragile, such as buds, blossom, children, laughter, jewellery, poetry and song. All these are things that human beings value and which are destroyed easily in a war. In contrast to these delicate things we have: hearts turned to stone; no more buds; burned mouths; charred bones; mirrors smashed by bombs; screams; and silence. This contrast between things of beauty and images of destruction is at the heart of the poem.

With a partner discuss:

1 how well you think this approach works. Is there a good balance between the horrors of war and the beautiful or fragile things? Refer to specific examples.

2 whether you think the poem could have been more forthright in its condemnation of war.

Boost Your Grade

This section, and others like it throughout the book, will help you turn your D grade work into C grades, and your B grade work into A grades.

The examiner's mark scheme for the mock questions is on page 32. On page 72 you will find a grid that will help you choose which poems to group together in your answers.

Assessing your answer

There are three Assessment Objectives for this part of the exam.

Candidates are required to demonstrate their ability to:

* read, with insight and engagement, making appropriate references to texts and developing and sustaining interpretation of them;

* select material appropriate to their purpose, collate material from different sources, and make cross references;

* understand and evaluate how writers use linguistic, structural and presentational devices to achieve their effects, and comment on ways language varies and changes.

Discuss these objectives with a partner. Make sure that you understand exactly what the examiners are expecting in your answers.

Which parts of the objectives do you find the most difficult? Share ways in which you try to cope with these requirements.

The Assessment Objectives describe in general terms what you should try to show in your answers.
For more detailed guidance, look at the examiner's mark scheme on page 32. How does this mark scheme relate to the Assessment Objectives that you have just studied?

Mark scheme for the mock questions

Skills		Content	
13–15 marks (notional D)	• some extended supported comment • range of comment supported by textual details • comment on effect(s) achieved by writer • awareness of feeling(s), attitude(s) and ideas	**13–18 marks**	• comments on language and other methods used to present the subject of the question, e.g. people, places, by means of detail from the poems • relevant comparison of methods of presentation/ language and their effects • personal response evident in comments demonstrating awareness/ understanding
16–18 marks (notional C)	• effective supporting use of textual detail • some cross reference • awareness of authorial techniques and purpose • understanding of feelings, attitudes and ideas		
19–21 marks (notional B)	• effective use of textual detail with integrated cross reference • understanding of a variety of writer's techniques • appreciation of feelings, attitudes and ideas	**19–27 marks**	• examination and analysis of methods used to present the subject of the question, e.g. people, places, in the two poems • examination and analysis of specific methods of presentation/specific uses of language, demonstrating their effects and effectiveness • integrated comparative approach, analysing and developing own response.
22–24 marks (notional A)	• references integrated with argument • analysis of a variety of writer's techniques • exploration of and empathy with writer's ideas and attitudes		
25–27 marks (notional A*)	• conceptualised response • close textual analysis • consistent insight and convincing/imaginative interpretation.		

Getting a Grade C

MOCK QUESTION 1

Compare the ways in which the poets present people in "Two Scavengers in a Truck" and <u>one</u> other poem of your choice from this selection.

Write about:

- what the different people are like
- what the poets think about them
- how the language brings out what the people are like
- how the language shows what the poets think about the people
- which poem you prefer and why.

Planning and structuring your response

It is vital that you plan your response before you begin writing. In this way, you will ensure that you have a focused and well-structured argument, rather than a series of unconnected points.

Consider the above question. In order to answer it, you need to look at the "ways" the poets use to present the people in the poems. This tells you that the examiners are just as interested in the way that poets express themselves as in what they express. Most people find writing about the content of a poem relatively easy, so it is the more difficult discussion of the poet's techniques that is rewarded with the best grades.

The grid below and on page 34 will help you think about what you need to focus on if you choose "Night of the Scorpion" as your second poem. Copy the grid and fill it in, adding to it if necessary. Construct your own grid if you choose a different poem.

What	How	Evidence
Two Scavengers in a Truck		
American people	Vocabulary used	Grungy/garbage/stoplight etc
"Scavengers" have a dirty job with anti-social hours	Description	
Scavengers' clothes and work conditions are unpleasant	Description	"bright yellow garbage truck" "red plastic blazers"
"Beautiful people" are rich and well-paid	Description	
Democracy is no guarantee of equal opportunities for all	Metaphor	"the high seas/of this democracy"

What	How	Evidence
Night of the Scorpion		
Village culture	Description	"Mud-baked walls"
Hindu beliefs	Neighbours' words	"May your suffering decrease/the misfortunes of your next birth"
Superstitious beliefs	Neighbours' words	
Peasants/neighbours annoying	Simile	"like swarms of flies"
Father in a panic	Description	
Senseless and desperate energy of father and peasants	Structure of the poem	The irregular lines (use of enjambment) add to the sense of chaos – as does the length of the first stanza
Peasants/neighbours talk a lot	Repetition	
Calm and common sense of the mother	Structure of the poem	The brevity of the final stanza

Analysing sample responses

Below are the first paragraphs of two responses to this question. The first is a grade D and the second is a grade C. Show why the essays have been awarded these grades by indicating where they fulfil the examiner's assessment criteria (see page 32). One example has been given in each case. How could you turn the grade D extract into a grade C?

1

In this essay, I will look at the way people are presented in the two poems, "Two Scavengers in a Truck" and "Night of the Scorpion". Both poems contain descriptions of a time and a place on which the poet is commenting. The way the people are described tells us about what the poet is trying to say about the situations - so it's important to look closely.

The "Two scavengers in a Truck" are garbage men on their way home from their "grungy" job. While they are stopped at traffic lights, they are next to a rich couple in an expensive car and the differences between the people is what Ferlinghetti writes about. "In Night of the Scorpion", the poet's mother has been stung and is in pain and might die. The poem seems to be about the way that the neighbours try to cure her of the sting. The way the villagers react to the sting is interesting because they have strong beliefs but don't really help.

The scavengers are dressed in "red plastic blazers" which sound horrible and cheap. The couple are dressed expensively. The man is wearing a "hip three piece linen suit" and the woman is wearing "a short skirt and coloured stockings". "The people in "Night of the Scorpion" are described in a different way because we do not know what they look like. We only know that the peasants were like "swarms of flies" and said a lot of prayers. This seems to say that there were not very helpful.

comment on effect(s) achieved by writer

2

I intend to compare and contrast the different ways in which people are presented in "Two Scavengers in a Truck" by Lawrence Ferlinghetti and "Night of the Scorpion" by Nissim Ezekiel. Both poets present a specific event – it is the way that the people in these events are depicted that allows the reader to understand what the poets are trying to say.

In the Ferlinghetti poem, two garbage men (described as "scavengers") are stopped at traffic lights next to a young successful couple in "an elegant open Mercedes". It is the differences between the two sets of people that seem to interest the poet. The world in which the "elegant couple" live is very different to that which the scavengers live in, although they live in the same country with the same laws. In "Night of the Scorpion", the poet's mother has been stung and is seriously ill. Ezekiel seems more interested in the belief of the people around her ("who buzzed the name of God a hundred times to paralyse the Evil One") that she can be saved by prayer.

One big difference between the two poems is that in "Two Scavengers in a Truck, Two Beautiful People in a Mercedes" the poet does not talk about what the characters do or what they might say, just what they look like, while "Night of the Scorpion" is interested in what the people in the poem believe and what they say and do. Although the poets are trying to say something about the people and what it's like to live where they do, they do it in different ways.

awareness of authorial techniques and purpose

Over to you ...

Now answer the question yourself, with your own choice of poems, bearing in mind the things that you need to do to score a Grade C. Make sure that you spend no longer than 45 minutes on it.

The Exam Skills Focus section on page 36 and at other points in this book will help you with your response.

EXAM SKILLS FOCUS – Writing an opening paragraph

The opening paragraph of an exam essay is always a little nerve-wracking for candidates – and it is a continuing source of irritation to examiners. Below are some of the common complaints made by examiners:

- **No opening paragraph at all** – essay started with no introduction
- **Too much 'writing in'** – didn't start making any relevant points until the end of the first page.
- **Confused** – didn't refer to the question
- **Overlong** – spent too much time saying what the essay was going to be about
- **Poorly organised** – didn't give a clear idea of how the essay would answer the question
- **Irrelevant** – didn't refer to the question, or to the poems to be considered, or to the points made later in the essay
- **Convoluted** – too complicated for its own good
- **Overambitious** – tried to include too much.

1 Discuss this list with a partner. Judging from the examiners' complaints, what should a good first paragraph be like?

2 Make a four-point list of your conclusions.

3 Share your list with the rest of the class and agree on a whole-class four-point list.

4 Use your list to assess the quality of the following opening paragraphs.

(a) In this essay I am going to discuss the way people are presented in "Night of the Scorpion" by Nissim Ezekiel and "Two Scavengers in a Truck" by Lawrence Ferlinghetti. In order to do this I am going to look at the content of each poem and discuss the way the two poets have chosen to explore how people's actions and appearances tell us about the cultures they live in. I will then write about their choice of language and the other literary techniques they employ. Finally I will discuss the impact of both poems on the reader.

(b) "Two Scavengers in a Truck" by Lawrence Ferlinghetti is about two different sets of people who are stopped at traffic lights in America. "Night of the Scorpion" by Nissim is about how people respond to the poet's mother being stung by a scorpion and the danger she faces.

(c) "Two Scavengers in a Truck", by Ferlinghetti and "Night of the Scorpion" by Ezekiel both have interesting things to say abut people and their beliefs. Both poems explore different cultural attitudes. They also have different approaches to their topics and they make their points in interesting ways.

5 Write a good opening paragraph for this essay topic.

Getting a Grade C

Compare "Nothing's Changed" with <u>one</u> other poem, showing how the poets reveal their ideas and feelings about the particular cultures they are writing about.

Write about:

- what their ideas are about the culture or cultures
- what their feelings are about the culture or cultures
- the methods they use to reveal their ideas and feelings.

Planning and structuring your response

Before tackling the question, you should decide on the points you want to make and the order you wish to present them. The most important word in the question is "how". An examination of the ways in which the poets achieve their effects will score more highly than simply describing what happens in each poem.

The grid below will help you think about what you need to focus on if you choose "Blessing" as your second poem. Copy the grid and fill it in, adding to it if necessary. Construct your own grid if you choose a different poem to compare with "Nothing's Changed".

What	How	Evidence
Nothing's Changed		
Set in South Africa	Place names/vocabulary	"District Six" "bunny chows"
Vast difference between rich and poor	Contrast (in restaurants)	
District Six should still belong to its mixed-race residents	Imagery/description	The "whites only inn" now "squats" in the area
The poet is angry	Statement and repetition (lines 12-16)	
Post-apartheid South Africa is a land of unofficial but real divisions	Symbolism	Glass, a transparent (yet physical) barrier, is mentioned five times in the poem. Poet wants to smash it
Blessing		
Set in a poor community suffering from drought	Simile + statement	"The skin cracks like a pod./ There is never enough water"
Water is seen as a blessing	Metaphors	
The water supply is uneven and unreliable	Shape of the poem	The varying length of the stanzas represents the change from "drip" to "flow"
The burst water pipe generates great excitement	Length of sentences	

Analysing a sample response

With a partner read the opening three paragraphs of the essay below and decide on the grade you would award it. Make sure that you can back up what you say with reference to the assessment criteria on page 32.

I intend to look at "Nothing's Changed" by Tatamkhulu Afrika and "Blessing" by Imtiaz Dharker to compare the ways in which the poets reveal what they feel about the different cultures they are writing about. Both poets tell us things about what they are worried about in their society and although the poems are about different countries, there are some things about them that are similar. This seems to be that there are too many poor people in the countries.

Afrika's poem is set in Cape Town after apartheid. The poet is walking in an area called District Six when he comes across a "new, up-market, haute cuisine" inn which he knows is for "whites only" although there is no sign any more. This is because the restaurant is too expensive for the black people to eat there. "Down the road", there is a café for the "working man" where there are plastic top tables and people wipe their hands on their jeans. Afrika is angry that he feels like a boy again, looking at what the rich people have, even when apartheid has finished. I know this because his "hands are burning for a stone, a bomb" to break the glass. Afrika's idea about his culture is that although some things have changed in South Africa, the people who had no money before still have no money.

In the poem by Imtiaz Dharker, the "Blessing" is when a water pipe bursts and allows people to collect it in "pots" and "buckets". It is set in India where there are people living in slums. We know from the first lines that "there is never enough water". The people in the poem are very excited by what has happened and a crowd gathers on the street. They feel that a "kindly god" has made the pipe burst but they do not understand that it is accidents like these that are the reason why there is never enough water. Although the people are happy, this is not really a good thing at all and will lead to more problems later. Dharker seems to be worried about the health of the people in the slums – especially the children with "small bones".

When you have decided on the grade you would award this extract, make a list of its strengths and weaknesses. What needs to be improved?

Over to you ...

Now tackle the question on your own, with your own choice of poems, ensuring that you spend no longer than 45 minutes on it.

The Exam Skills Focus section on page 39 and at other points in this book will help you with your response.

EXAM SKILLS FOCUS – Expressing degrees of certainty

Poets often express their views indirectly, so it is usually necessary for you to interpret what they have to say. This means that you will often have to express your own ideas with varying degrees of certainty. Words and phrases that you could use to express uncertainty are:

- perhaps
- suggests
- maybe
- implies
- could mean ...
- seems to ...

1 **Below is part of a discussion of "Nothing's Changed". Read it through and indicate the words that express the degree of certainty of the comment.**

In the early part of the poem the description of 'seeding grasses' and cans underfoot suggests a run down and neglected landscape. In the case of the "amiable weeds", the meaning is not clear. The words are in conflict as "amiable" implies friendliness whilst "weeds" indicates neglect and decay. The phrase could mean that the weeds are clustering round like a group of friends, or the sense of "amiable" might be "not doing anybody any harm". Later in the poem Tatamkhulu Afrika is much more assertive.

Hands burn
for a stone, a bomb

clearly indicates the degree of his anger and the final sentence of the poem expresses his frustration under the new regime in South Africa.

2 Write a similar paragraph about "Blessing".

3 Swap your work with a partner's and highlight the words expressing degrees of certainty.

Getting a Grade A

MOCK QUESTION 1

Compare "Limbo" with one other poem where you think the writer reveals strong feelings about a culture or tradition.

Planning and structuring your response

It is vital that you plan your response before you begin writing. In this way, you will ensure that you have a focused and well-structured argument, rather than a series of unconnected points.

When planning your response, it's important to look at the ways in which the poets express what they have to say and how they use language to do it. Remember that you mustn't simply write about the content of the poem but analyse the techniques used and the effects created by the language used.

The grid below will help you think about what you need to focus on if you choose "What Were They Like?" as your second poem. Copy the grid and fill it in, adding to it if necessary. Construct your own grid if you choose a different poem to compare with "Limbo".

What	How	Evidence
Limbo		
Representation of limbo dance on the page	Description + musical rhythm of the poem	
Two separate stories going on in the poem	Mixture of threatening and celebratory images	"the dark deck is slavery" "the drummers are praising me"
The painful arching of the back to go under the stick is compared to going into the hold of a slave ship	Extended metaphor	
Successfully performing a limbo dance is likened to surviving the Middle Passage	Extended metaphor	"out of the dark/and the dumb gods are raising me/up/up/up"
Poem is a celebration of West Indian culture	Imagery at end of the poem	
What Were They Like?		
The Vietnamese were completely destroyed	Structure of poem	Questions and answers about a past culture
Peasants of Vietnam were a gentle people	Detail in the answers	
They led a simple, natural life	Descriptions and images from nature	"gardens", "blossoms", "buds", "moths"
Their annihilation was horrific	Contrast of the images of peace and destruction	

Analysing sample responses

Below are the opening paragraphs of two responses to this question. The first is a grade B and the second a grade A. Show why the essays have been awarded these grades by indicating where they fulfil the examiner's assessment criteria (see page 32). One example has been given in each case. How could you turn the grade B extract into a grade A?

1

I shall look at the way Edward Kamau Brathwaite and Denise Levertov use language to express their feelings about the cultures they are writing about. I will examine what they are saying about the cultures and the poetic techniques they use to do so.

In "Limbo" Kamau Brathwaite looks at the limbo dance and what it actually means. There seems to be two different things going on in the poem at once. The first is a limbo dancer performing the dance with the aid of drummers in the background who are "calling" and "praising" him while the second has more sinister undertones as it refers to the "dark deck" of slavery and recalls the passage of Africans in the slave ships on their way to the Caribbean.

The rhythm of the drums is heard in the poem which has a very strong beat due to the repetition in the mostly short lines. There is also a chorus, emphasizing the sense of performance:

limbo

limbo like me

The beat helps to visualise the dance but the words often seem to mean more than one thing. For example the "stick" can be the bar under which the dancer must pass or the stick with which the slaves would have been beaten. The fact that these words can be taken to mean such different things suggests that Brathwaite is proud of the Caribbean culture, but also aware of the wrongs that have been done to his people.

> appreciation of feelings, attitudes and ideas

2

In this essay, I intend to compare "Limbo" with "What Were They Like?", analysing the ways in which the poets display their feelings about the cultures they write about.

"Limbo" by Kamau Brathwaite concerns limbo dancing (as well as connotations of the word 'limbo') – considering it both as a spectacle that tourists to the Caribbean might expect to see and as a metaphor for the Middle Passage – the route via which Africans were transported as slaves to the Americas. The limbo reportedly originated on the slave ships in order to keep the "cargo" fit and healthy and is

Continued ▼▼▼

now a traditional Caribbean dance. Brathwaite's poem considers the origins of the dance at the same time as describing a modern performance. Many of the words he uses can be interpreted in different ways. For example if you look at the line "And limbo stick is the silence in front of me", it can be seen as the literal limbo stick that the dancer must go under, while the "silence" can also be read as the fear of the slaves on the ships, who were ignorant of where they were being taken or whether they would survive the voyage. Their cultures and religions had also been "silenced" by the slave trade. The "stick" might represent the bar for the dance as well as the instrument that slave traders may have used as a weapon.

"Darkness" is another major theme in the poem and is linked to the "silence". On a simple level, it may mean that the dance is taking place at night but it also refers to a people who have had their lives thrown into darkness – not just the darkness of the hold of the ship where they were stored, but also the obscuring of their history and culture (the history of the period would have been written by Europeans). Brathwaite seems to be celebrating the fact that in spite of the horrors of slavery, many of the customs have survived. Their gods had been rendered "dumb" by the transportation but the dance lifts them "out of the dark". This is both the dancer rising up having gone under the bar and the resurgence of the cultures of those deported as slaves. Limbo has been a painful experience for the dancer and the people but Brathwaite is proud of his ancestry and its resilience.

references integrated
with argument

Over to you ...

Now answer the question yourself, with your own choice of poems, bearing in mind the things you need to do to score a grade A. Make sure that you spend no longer than 45 minutes on your answer.

The Exam Skills Focus section found on page 43 and at other points in this book will help you with your response.

EXAM SKILLS FOCUS – Comparing two poems

There are two different ways of approaching a comparison essay. You need to ⌐ method you are going to follow before you write your essay.

In the **first method** you:

1 introduce both poems and then relate them briefly to the subject of the question

2 focus on one poem, bringing out the points of theme, language and style that relate to the question

3 focus on the second poem in the same way, but this time discussing its similarity or contrast to the first poem for each point

4 conclude the essay, summarising the key points of comparison and contrast.

In the **second method** you:

1 introduce both poems and then relate them briefly to the subject of the question

2 focus on each aspect of the question in turn, referring to both poems as you go, so as to bring out the comparison or contrast

3 conclude the essay, summarising the key points of comparison and contrast.

For example, the paragraph below uses the second method to explore the way two poems deal with the past and present.

> The structure of Levertov's poem separates out the past and present; the questions ask about the past of the Vietnamese people whilst the answers reveal a bleak present in which much has been forgotten about a people who no longer exist. Brathwaite's poem would not have worked if it had taken this course. By interweaving the past and present, the joy of the dance is starkly contrasted with the horrors of slavery. The fact that the joy exists today having survived the horrors of the slave ships is part of the message of the poem.

The first method is more straightforward and allows you to focus on one poem at a time. However, it is less effective at bringing out the points of comparison and contrast.

The second method is a very effective way of analysing and comparing poems, but it is more difficult to carry off.

Use whichever method you prefer, but don't mix the two or your essay will be unbalanced and confused.

Mock Question 2

Compare the methods that <u>two</u> poets use in their poems to explore the past.

Planning and structuring your response

Before starting to write, it is important to plan your answer, working out the order of what you want to say.

To help you focus your thoughts, copy the grid below, which assumes you choose "Island Man" and "Vultures". Then fill it in, adding to it if necessary. Construct your own grid if you choose different poems.

What	How	Evidence
Island Man		
The Caribbean Man dreams of his past	Stated in stanza 1	He "wakes up to the sound of blue surf in his head"
Image of the past is very comfortable and pleasant	Description	
Island Man wants to cling to this vision	Repetition of sounds imply someone being dragged unwillingly from sleep	"groggily groggily", "muffling, muffling"
Vultures		
Poem begins in the present	Description of the vultures' behaviour	
Poem may have been written in response to the Biafran war	Hinted at by image in description	"corpse in a water-logged trench"
Poet's theories of evil are then transferred to the Second World War	Reference to Belsen prison camp	
Final lines of the poem are set outside of time	General statement	

Analysing a sample answer

With a partner, read the opening paragraphs of the essay on page 45 and decide on the grade you would award it. Make sure that you back up what you say with reference to the assessment criteria on page 32.

In "Island Man" by Grace Nichols and "Vultures" by Chinua Achebe, the past is referred to in very different ways, both in terms of the ways in which it is presented and the way the poets seem to feel about it.

In "Island Man", the past is something that has become idealised. The Island Man is homesick for the things in the Caribbean that he most misses, namely the "sound of the blue surf", "the wild seabirds" and "the sun breaking defiantly" on "the small emerald isle". The way in which the Caribbean island is described sounds much like something out of a travel brochure, conjuring images of unspoilt beaches, abundant wildlife and pleasant weather, contrasting vividly with the "grey metallic soar" of the London North Circular which seems to indicate traffic jams of people on their way to work. It's actually unlikely that life on a Caribbean island is as perfect as it's depicted or that London is as unpleasant as the "dull roar" of the traffic sounds. The fact that Nichols uses a dream to present the past of the Island Man is significant as it underlines the idealistic nature of the vision. When people look back on the past, it is perhaps fortunate that on the whole we remember more good things than bad. The scene painted of the Caribbean island appears to be a fond reminiscence.

The past (and indeed time in general) is treated very differently in Achebe's poem. Rather than show the transition of a few seconds from a pleasant dream to a more stark reality, "Vultures" concerns the nature of evil. The poem begins by describing the birds "nestled close" to one another having just "picked the eyes of a swollen corpse", showing that love and affection can exist in the most gruesome scenarios. We are not given a date for this but it seems likely that it was something that Achebe might have seen during the Biafran War in Nigeria in the late 1960s. By comparing the activities of vultures with those of the Commandant at Belsen in World War II, we can see that the poet is making an observation on human nature in general that is not dependent on time. The poet could have chosen men who have committed atrocities from many other wars over the ages without affecting the impact of the poem. Those responsible for genocides may still show touching concern for their "tender offspring". Time is irrelevant in "Vultures" as the past is something that serves to show that human nature doesn't change.

When you have decided on the grade you would award this extract, make a list of its strengths and weaknesses. What needs to be improved?

Over to you ...

Now tackle the question on your own, with your own choice of poems, ensuring that you spend no longer than 45 minutes on it.

The Exam Skills Focus section on page 46 and at other points in this book will help you with your response.

EXAM SKILLS FOCUS – Textual detail and references

According to the examiner's assessment criteria, B grade answers show "effective use of textual detail with integrated cross reference", whereas A grade answers show "references integrated with argument" (see page 32).

Talk with a partner about what you understand the difference between these two criteria to be. What is the difference between referring to the poems by quoting in detail from the text, and integrating references to the text **with your argument**?

Here and on page 47 are two examples of responses to mock question 2. Look at how each of them refers to and quotes from the poems. Which of them would you give an A grade to, and which a B? Be prepared to justify your decision to the rest of the class.

Grace Nichols and Chinua Achebe explore the past in very different ways in the "Island Man" and "Vultures". "Island Man" is a poem that describes a few seconds of somebody's life, giving a glimpse of where they are living now and where they were brought up, while "Vultures" is a poem that looks at evil and how it has always been present in people.

"Vultures" refers to a time from the past but you get the feeling that it could have referred to many other times to have made the same point. Achebe gives the example of how the "Commandant at Belsen" might have bought sweets for his daughter having just overseen slaughter in a concentration camp, meaning that he is able to do horrific things at the same time as acting like a loving parent. In the same way, the vultures are able to be affectionate to each other after having eaten the eyes of a "swollen corpse". The poet obviously thinks that people act in the same way and uses the actions of the vultures as a metaphor for this. His observation of the vultures appears to be in the present, while the camp at Belsen was during the Second World War. The presentation therefore links evil in the past with evil in the present. The last eleven lines of the poem are the conclusions that he draws from what he has seen and learned.

"Island Man" is a poem that contrasts the reality of the present with a (literally) dreamlike vision of the past. Island Man was originally from a Caribbean island but has moved to London where the "roar" of the traffic is compared to the natural beauty and sunshine of the "emerald island" where he was born. The past seems very attractive to the man and the way he remembers it sounds like a holiday brochure. This is very different to the way in which London is described.

"Island Man" describes the process of waking up from a dream about the past and having to face a decidedly less attractive reality. The "steady breaking and wombing" of the sea lapping on the shore and the "sun surfacing defiantly in the east" are replaced by the sounds:

of grey metallic soar
                    to surge of wheels
to dull north circular roar.

The "wild seabirds" and "emerald isle" represent the way that he remembers the Caribbean island, with all its peace, quiet and natural beauty. These images are replaced with grinding mechanical sounds indicating cars and pollution. The adjectives "grey" and "dull" also emphasize that it's likely to be an overcast, perhaps even wintry, morning in London with the roads full of commuters on their way to work. The desire of the Island Man to return to the past is not stated in the poem but seems likely as the "sound of blue surf in his head" is associated with the comforts of sleep from which he is pulled "groggily groggily".

"Vultures" is a poem that deals with the past (and time in general) in a very different way. Unlike "Island Man" which is a slight poem covering a very short time span, Achebe is commenting on an aspect of human behaviour that he believes to have been ever present – the ability of "even an ogre" to show love to his family while committing atrocities elsewhere. The poem begins with an observation from the present and then gives a theoretical example from the Second World War of the "Commandant at Belsen" who will "pick up a chocolate for his tender offspring" and ends with the ambiguous conclusion on how "the perpetuity of evil" can be viewed.

Author profile

Sujata Bhatt was born in Ahmedabad (India) in 1956 and was initially brought up in Poona. She was educated in New Orleans and later Connecticut. She now lives in Germany with her husband. Her mother tongue is Gujerati although she writes in English.

from "Search for My Tongue"

You ask me what I mean
by saying I have lost my tongue.
I ask you, what would you do
if you had two tongues in your mouth,
5 and lost the first one, the mother tongue,
and could not really know the other,
the foreign tongue.
You could not use them both together
even if you thought that way.
10 And if you lived in a place you had to
speak a foreign tongue,
your mother tongue would rot,
rot and die in your mouth
until you had to spit it out.
15 I thought I spit it out
but overnight while I dream,

મને હતું કે આખ્ખી જીભ આખ્ખી ભાષા,

(munay hutoo kay aakhee jeebh aakhee bhasha)

મેં થૂં કી નાખી છે.

20 (may thoonky nakhi chay)

પરં તુ રાત્રે સ્વપ્નામાં મારી ભાષા પાછી આવે છે.

(parantoo rattray svupnama mari bhasha pachi aavay chay)

ફૂલની જેમ મારી ભાષા મારી જીભ

(foolnee jaim mari bhasha mari jeebh)

25 મોઢામાં ખીલે છે.

(modhama kheelay chay)

ફૂલની જેમ મારી ભાષા મારી જીભ

(fullnee jaim mari bhasha mari jeebh)

મોઢામાં પાકે છે.

30 (modhama pakay chay)

it grows back, a stump of a shoot
grows longer, grows moist, grows strong veins
it ties the other tongue in knots,
the bud opens, the bud opens in my mouth,
35 it pushes the other tongue aside.
Everytime I think I've forgotten,
I think I've lost the mother tongue,
it blossoms out of my mouth.

Sujata Bhatt

Making sense of the poem

1 Use a table like the one below to record your thoughts about the poem.

Line or word	Thoughts
You ask me what I mean by saying I have lost my tongue	Speaker is addressing someone who doesn't seem to understand what s/he's talking about. Speaker feels alone.
I ask you, what would you do if you had two tongues in your mouth	Tongue is being used to mean both language and the physical organ in the mouth

2 Compare your thoughts with those of a partner. Are there any significant differences?

3 Write down in a sentence or two what you think is happening in the poem.

BACKGROUND

While living in America, Sujata Bhatt read a great deal of both Eastern and Western poetry; she was herself a quite prolific poet in her teens. But she said in an interview that although she had studied a wide selection of different poets, she "felt that no one really spoke for me, no one had a life as strangely disjointed as mine – and so I felt alone in my writing, I felt that my writing did not 'fit' in with either the Eastern or Western tradition. The poem 'Search for my Tongue' grew out of this feeling."

The purpose of the poem

1 With a partner think about:

- the point the poet is trying to make.
- how the content of the poem helps to make this point.

2 The return of Sujata Bhatt's mother tongue, Gujerati, is reported first of all in script, then in transliterated form (in brackets). Do you think including a section that most English readers will not be able to understand is a good idea? Give your reasons.

3 Why do you think Sujata Bhatt took the risk of confusing her readers here? How is it appropriate, given the subject of the poem and the point she is making?

The poet's approach

1 **The poem seems to be a dramatic monologue.**

   - Who do you think the speaker is talking to?

   - How does this both suit the subject of the poem and help the poet to convey her feelings

2 **Sujata Bhatt uses some powerful imagery to express her feelings in this poem. Look at lines 12–15.**

   - Why do you think Sujata Bhatt has chosen this image to describe the loss of her original language?

   - What kind of images does the poet use to describe the return of her mother tongue? Why do you think this choice of imagery is appropriate? How do the two sets of ideas work together?

   - What does the idea of the tongue rotting inside the mouth suggest to you about the poet's attitude or feelings?

Gathering your thoughts

This poem is a very personal exploration of the effect of living in a foreign country and constantly speaking a foreign tongue.

1 **How well do you think Sujata Bhatt has conveyed the strength of her feelings?**

2 **How has it helped you to understand the experience of someone who has had to adopt a new language?**

3 **Does it make you realise anything about your own language and how that is linked to your identity?**

Tom Leonard was born in 1944 in Glasgow, where he still lives; his poetry is written in the dialect of the Glasgow area. He writes about the snobbery of people (especially in literary circles) who believe that people who don't speak (and write) the "Queen's English" are to be looked down on.

from "Unrelated Incidents"

this is thi
six a clock
news thi
man said n
5 thi reason
a talk wia
BBC accent
iz coz yi
widny wahnt
10 mi ti talk
aboot thi
trooth wia
voice lik
wanna yoo
15 scruff. if
a toktaboot
thi trooth
lik wanna yoo
scruff yi
20 widny thingk
it wuz troo.
jist wonna yoo
scruff tokn.
thirza right
25 way ti spell
ana right way
ti tok it. this
is me tokn yir
right way a
30 spellin. this

is ma trooth
yooz doant no
thi trooth
yirsellz cawz
35 yi canny talk
right. this is
the six a clock
nyooz. belt up.

Tom Leonard

Making sense of the poem

First of all you need to work out what is going on in the poem.

For this poem your thoughts might go something like this.

> So ... it's a news bulletin. But why the non-standard spelling?

> widny – sounds Scottish – so does avoot – must be a news bulletin in a regional accent. As opposed to a 'normal' BBC accent.

> wanna yoo scruff – not very polite. Is it attacking the people who listen to the news?

> Seems to be getting at people's attitude to strong accents – don't trust them?

> People wouldn't believe the news if it was spoken in everyday speech?

> Connection here between 'correct' speech and 'correct' spelling – explains odd spelling – no capital letters either.

> Newsreader claims that you have to be able to talk properly to speak the truth – ordinary people who can't speak 'correctly' don't know the truth.

> belt up. Newsreader not interested in what ordinary people have to say. Just in his own words. Attack on newsreaders and 'proper' accents – not on listeners.

1 With a partner discuss whether your thoughts on the poem were similar to the ones in the bubbles. What other thoughts did you have?

2 Look carefully at the suggested thoughts in the bubbles. Do they change as the reading of the poem progresses?

3 Write down a sentence or two about what you think is happening in the poem.

BACKGROUND

On his website, Tom Leonard writes:

"All modes of speech are valid – upper-class, middle-class, working-class, from whatever region: linguistic chauvinism [considering one way of speaking to be better than another] is a drag, pre-judging people just because they speak 'rough' or with the accent of another region, or equally, pre-judging people just because they speak 'posh'. But to have created, or at least to have preserved, a particular mode of pronunciation on a strictly economic base, cannot but have very deep repercussions in a society, and in the literature of a society.

When you have in a society on the one hand a standardised literary grammar (standardised spelling and standardised syntax) and on the other hand a standardised mode of pronunciation, the notion tends to get embedded in the consciousness of that society that one is part of the essence of the other. Prescriptive grammar, in other words, becomes the sound made flesh of prescriptive pronunciation. The tawdry little syllogism [argument] goes something like this:

1. In speaking of reality, there is a standard correct mode of pronunciation.

2. In writing of reality, there is a standard correct mode of pronunciation.

3. Therefore in reality, correct spelling and correct syntax are synonymous [associated] with correct pronunciation."

The purpose of the poem

Once you have established **what** is happening in the poem you can then go on to ask yourself **why** the poem is as it is. This process will be different for every poem you study but you need to consider two basic questions.

- What point is the poet trying to make?
- How does the content of the poem help to make this point?

1 Work with a partner to gather your ideas in order to answer these two questions. Start by looking at the list of statements below and deciding which you agree with and which you think are wrong or need adapting. You will probably be able to add ideas of your own.

- The poet wants to express his anger at people's prejudice.
- The poet wants to make his readers think about their attitudes towards regional dialects and accents.
- The poet believes that there is a correct way of speaking that is better than other ways.
- The poet is attacking the BBC for its attitude towards dialects and accents.

2 Once you have decided on the point(s) the poet is making, select evidence from the poem that supports your idea. Consider:

- the poet's choice of speaker and situation
- the arguments used by the speaker.

3 Do you agree with Tom Leonard's basic point? Are people judged as much for the way they speak as for what they say? Give reasons for your views.

4 Why do you think Tom Leonard frames his ideas in the form of a news bulletin? Do you think these ideas explain the way people speak on television? Discuss your thoughts with a partner.

The poet's approach

Here the two fundamental questions you need to ask are:

- What is the effect of the poet's choices about **language**?
- How does the **form** of the poem help to make its overall point?

1 Before looking at these, discuss as a class what you expect when you hear the news presented. What conventions are followed by newsreaders?

2 How does this poem subvert, or break, these conventions? What do you think the effect of this is on the reader?

LANGUAGE

1 List, with examples, the different ways in which the language of the poem departs from standard English.

2 Why has the poet chosen to write it like this? What would be lost if it were in standard English? Could it have been written in standard English?

3 How would you describe the speaker's tone of voice? Which words or sentences particularly help you to understand the speaker's tone of voice and attitude?

Tom Leonard's most important and obvious choice was to write the poem in a way that reflects his own Glaswegian accent. There is a slight risk that people might find this off-putting, but his use of phonetic spelling and short, simple sentences ensures that his meaning is clear after a few readings. Any risk in this area is more than outweighed by the powerful and unusual effect he achieves. Everyone knows what to expect from a news bulletin and to present it with such unusual spelling, and therefore pronunciation, is very striking. His main point about how people respond to accents comes across very strongly when readers of the poem have to adopt a regional accent to read it correctly.

4 Do you think the risks Tom Leonard has taken using non standard English in this poem are worth it in terms of increased impact?

FORM

Look now at the form and structure of the poem.

1 What do you notice about the length of the sentences and the effect this has?

2 Why do you think there are no stanzas in the poem?

3 What effect does the final sentence have?

4 With a partner discuss whether you think Tom Leonard has communicated his ideas effectively. Consider all the points in the sections 'Language' and 'Form' above.

Gathering your thoughts

The issue of language is clearly very important in this poem. Tom Leonard objects to the assumption that people who speak properly have greater access to the truth than people who use a regional accent. In many ways the poem demonstrates, through its use of a regional accent, that the very opposite is the case. The poem encourages us to think about social attitudes to accent and class through its use of an interesting and unusual form.

1 Do you think there has been any change in attitudes to accent and class since the poem was written?

John Agard was born in Guyana in 1949 and is himself of mixed parentage. He lived in the capital city, Georgetown, before moving to England in 1977, where his father had settled. He worked for the Commonwealth Institute for many years giving talks and workshops. He lives in Surrey and works as a freelance writer and performer of poetry.

Half-Caste

Excuse me
standing on one leg
I'm half-caste

Explain yuself
5 wha yu mean
when yu say half-caste
yu mean when picasso
mix red an green
is a half-caste canvas/
10 explain yuself
wha yu mean
when yu say half-caste
yu mean when light an shadow
mix in de sky
15 is a half-caste weather/
well in dat case
england weather
nearly always half-caste
in fact some o dem cloud
20 half-caste til dem overcast
so spiteful dem dont want de sun pass
ah rass/
explain yuself
wha yu mean
25 when yu say half-caste
yu mean tchaikovsky
sit down at dah piano
an mix a black key
wid a white key
30 is a half-caste symphony/

Explain yuself
wha yu mean
Ah listening to yu wid de keen
half of mih ear
35 Ah lookin at yu wid de keen
half of mih eye
and when I'm introduced to yu

I'm sure you'll understand
why I offer yu half-a-hand
40 an when I sleep at night
I close half-a-eye
consequently when I dream
I dream half-a-dream
an when moon begin to glow
45 I half-caste human being
cast half-a-shadow
but yu must come back tomorrow
wid de whole of yu eye
an de whole of yu ear
50 an de whole of yu mind

an I will tell yu
de other half
of my story

John Agard

Making sense of the poem

Use a table like the one below to record your thoughts about this poem.

Line or word	Thoughts
Excuse me standing on one leg i'm half-caste	This doesn't make sense- why should someone stand on one leg because they are half-caste? Surprising opening. Humour? Who is speaking? Half-caste not politically correct nowadays - old poem?
Explain yuself	Yuself - non standard English. Is this another voice? Talking to the half-caste?

1 Compare your thoughts with those of a partner. Are there are any significant differences?

2 Write down in a sentence or two what you think is happening in the poem.

The purpose of the poem

1 What point is the poet trying to make?

2 How does the content of the poem help to make this point?

3 What does John Agard think of people who call themselves or other people "half-caste"? Why do you think he would prefer the term "mixed race"?

4 How does he use humour to make his point?

The poet's approach

1 With a partner consider:
  • What is the effect of the poet's choices about language? (Find as many ways as you can of how the poem departs from standard English.)
  • How would you describe the poet's attitude and tone of voice?
  • Which aspects of the poem indicate that it is intended to be read aloud?
  • How does the form of the poem help to make its overall point? For example, look at:
    – phrases that are repeated and the effect of this
    – patterns or groups of ideas that the poet establishes
    – how the poet begins and ends the poem – what does the whole poem represent?

2 This poem is about taking pride in yourself. How is this reflected in John Agard's use of non-standard English?

John Agard repeats the request:

> Explain yuself
> wha yu mean
> when yu say half-caste

three times in the poem and each time follows it with an example of mixing. This repetition helps to hold the poem together and allows him to explore the same idea in a variety of ways.

3 Look carefully at the examples John Agard gives of mixing – two of them are clearly beautiful. What do you make of his comments on the English weather?

Tip

Always look for patterns in poetry. Generally they hold poems together and there is nearly always a reason why a poet breaks a pattern that he or she has established.

John Agard uses "Explain yuself / wha yu mean" a fourth time in line 31, but here the pattern is broken and the poet moves on to make fun of the idea of half of anything in a human being.

4 Why do you think he repeats "de whole of yu" three times at the end of this section?

This poem seems to be a sort of conversation. The "half-caste" speaks first and then the poet attacks his use of the term "half-caste" first by looking at the idea of mixing and then by ridiculing the idea of half of anything.

5 What do you think is the point being made in the last three lines?

Gathering your thoughts

This poem is a meditation on the term "half-caste".

1 Why do you think John Agard has chosen to attack people who use it to describe themselves?

2 How effective do you think the poet has been in getting his point across? Why does the use of humour help?

Poems from Different Cultures and Traditions   CLUSTER 2

57

Author profile

Derek Walcott is a Nobel Prize winning poet and playwright. He was born in 1930 in Saint Lucia, West Indies, to an English father and an African mother.

In his works Walcott has studied the conflict between the heritage of European and West Indian culture, the long road from slavery to independence, and his own role as a nomad between the cultures. He has written both in standard English and in West Indian dialect.

Love after Love

The time will come
When, with elation,
You will greet yourself arriving
At your own door, in your own mirror,
5 And each will smile at the other's welcome,

And say sit here. Eat.
You will love again the stranger who was your self.
Give wine. Give bread. Give back your heart
To itself, to the stranger who has loved you

10 All your life, whom you ignored
For another, who knows you by heart.
Take down the love-letters from the bookshelf,

The photographs, the desperate notes,
Peel your images from the mirror.
15 Sit. Feast on your life.

Derek Walcott

Making sense of the poem

This poem contains elements of fantasy as well as its more serious point.

1 What impossible things are suggested in the poem?

2 The title of the poem refers to an earlier love – who was this directed towards?

3 According to Derek Walcott, what kind of love should come afterwards?

4 What is the situation of the person addressed in the poem?

5 Write a sentence which sums up the point the poem is making about old age.

6 What do the images of bread and wine suggest?

The purpose of the poem

There are many poems that describe the pain when a love affair is over, but in "Love after Love" Derek Walcott presents an optimistic picture of life after love. Walcott seems to be suggesting that we spend years being what other people want us to be. When this is no longer necessary, you can love "the stranger who was your self".

1 Do you find Derek Walcott's response to the end of a love affair or long-term relationship believable? Why?

2 Does the alternative kind of love sound appealing to you? Give your reasons.

3 Do you think his ideas apply particularly to old age, or is the poet making a general point?

The poet's approach

We can tell the mood of this poem by looking at Derek Walcott's choice of words. He talks of meeting yourself with great happiness or "elation" and he invites the reader to "feast" on his or her life. Instead of a lonely person thinking back on events we are given the image of a meeting or even a dinner party in which two aspects of the self look back fondly over old memories. The enthusiasm and warmth of this meeting is communicated through the frequent imperatives such as "Eat", "Give wine", "Sit" and, finally, "Feast". The final instruction is particularly noticeable as it contains the metaphorical instruction to "Feast on your life", as if your memories were sustaining in some way.

The other element in the poem is its use of a fantastic situation – meeting yourself – as a way of underlining the central idea.

Key Terms

The **mood** or **tone** of a poem is its general atmosphere or feeling. This might be anything from thoughtful to humorous; it is usually influenced by the poet's choice of words or situation.

1 What do you think of the idea of having two versions of yourself? Does it strike you as interesting or absurd? What would you gain from having a conversation with your own reflection in a mirror?

2 Look now at the structure of the poem. How has the poet arranged his ideas? Can you explain why he has started new stanzas where he has?

3 The poem uses different tenses as it shifts in time. Identify where the present, future and past tenses are used. Why is it appropriate that the poem ranges across these three different periods of time?

Gathering your thoughts

Derek Walcott's poem is a very personal one. It uses simple language and everyday situations to in order to reflect on a common human problem.

1 Other than the fact that the poem is by a Caribbean writer, is there anything to indicate that it represents a particular culture or tradition?

Imtiaz Dharker was born in Pakistan, grew up in Glasgow and now lives in Mumbai (formerly Bombay) in India. It is from this life of transitions that she draws her themes: childhood, exile, journeying, home and religious strife.

She works as a documentary film-maker and is also an artist, conceiving her books as sequences of poems and drawings.

This Room

This room is breaking out
of itself, cracking through
its own walls
in search of space, light,
5 empty air.

The bed is lifting out of
its nightmares.
From dark corners, chairs
are rising up to crash through clouds.

10 This is the time and place
to be alive:
when the daily furniture of our lives
stirs, when the improbable arrives.
Pots and pans bang together
15 in celebration, clang
past the crowd of garlic, onions, spices,
fly by the ceiling fan.
No one is looking for the door.

In all this excitement
20 I'm wondering where
I've left my feet, and why

my hands are outside, clapping.

Imtiaz Dharker

Making sense of the poem

"This Room" reveals its meaning slowly. At first it is unclear what is causing the disruption to the room.

1 How can you tell from the first two stanzas that the room has been an unhappy place?

2 At what point does it become clear that the room is bursting out of itself for a good reason?

3 What other images does Imtiaz Dharker use to convey a sense of joy?

4 Why is no one "looking for the door"?

5 With a partner consider what the poet means when she says that "the improbable arrives". Is it to do with what is happening to the room or with the cause of the celebration in the first place?

The purpose of the poem

Happiness is very difficult to describe.

1 How successful is Imtiaz Dharker in giving an impression of how the speaker feels?

2 Do you find it odd that she has not described the cause of her happiness?

The poet's approach

Although Imtiaz Dharker is primarily concerned with expressing a feeling, the context in which she writes is also communicated.

1 Jot down all the things in the room.

2 What does the fact that all these things are in the same room suggest about it?

The element of the improbable plays a major part in this poem.

- How can a room break "out of itself"?
- How might a bed lift "out of its nightmares"?
- How can someone lose contact with her hands and feet?

3 With a partner discuss whether these improbable ideas communicate the speaker's feelings effectively.

Gathering your thoughts

Imtiaz Dharker writes from a particular social and economic perspective. She expresses joy from the point of view of a person whose whole life seems to be conducted in one room.

1 Do you think this perspective affects the overall impact of the poem? How?

2 The room seems like a restrictive place at first. What is the effect on the person who lives there of the room bursting into life?

Niyi Osundare is a poet and a professor at Nigeria's oldest university, the University of Ibadan, although he started as a "farmer born, peasant-bred" oral singer. He sees himself in the tradition of the town-crier, the voice which carries a message to the people. Much of his work concerns the many exploitations of Africa, both of the raw materials of the land and the ideals of the people.

Not My Business

They picked Akanni up one morning
Beat him soft like clay
And stuffed him down the belly
Of a waiting jeep.
5   What business of mine is it
     So long they don't take the yam
     From my savouring mouth?

They came one night
Booted the whole house awake
10 And dragged Danladi out,
Then off to a lengthy silence.
     What business of mine is it
     So long they don't take the yam
     From my savouring mouth?

15 Chinwe went to work one day
Only to find her job was gone:
No query, no warning, no probe –
Just one neat sack for a stainless record.
     What business of mine is it
20   So long they don't take the yam
     From my savouring mouth?

And then one evening
As I sat down to eat my yam
A knock on the door froze my hungry hand.
25 The jeep was waiting on my bewildered lawn
Waiting, waiting in its usual silence.

Niyi Osundare

Making sense of the poem

"Not My Business" tells the same story four times.

1 What is the story? How is the fourth version of the story different?

2 How has Niyi Osundare used the day to give a pattern to his different accounts?

3 Why do you think he has not arranged the accounts chronologically through a day?

Osundare is also known in Nigeria for his popular newspaper poetry column, and his outspoken critiques of successive military regimes. His use of the press as a vehicle for his art and ideas arises from his belief in the importance of communicating with ordinary people. While many writers, artists and academics were driven into exile by the country's military rulers, Osundare stayed to become a spokesman for the powerless and a witness for the oppressed.

The purpose of the poem

1 What would you say was the purpose of this poem?

2 Who is being criticised?

The poet's approach

This poem is probably one of the most formal in the collection. Each of the first three stanzas has a clear structure, consisting of four lines telling of the fate of a neighbour or acquaintance followed by a three-line chorus. This pattern is broken in the final stanza but many of the things mentioned earlier reoccur, including the time of day, eating a yam and the sinister jeep.

1 What is the effect of using this pattern? What do you expect to happen to the uncaring observer by the time you get to the end of the third stanza?

The poet's choice of language is significant throughout the poem. The jeep in the first stanza has a "belly", as if it were some hungry and unsavoury animal. You can see how effective this word is by examining alternatives to the word "belly".

2 Comment on how the first stanza would have read if Niyi Osundare had used "into the back" instead of "down the belly".

3 Why do you think there are so many references to hunger and food in the poem?

In the final stanza the language becomes even more intense. The phrases "froze my hungry hand" and "bewildered lawn" compress a great deal of meaning into a few words. They do this by placing an adjective that applies to a general situation in front of a noun. In these phrases the hand is not hungry and the lawn is not bewildered.

4 Find and discuss other examples of Osundare's careful word choice.

Gathering your thoughts

Niyi Osundare's poem is a warning about the dangers of looking out for your own self-interest and not being aware of the problems of others. People tend to ignore warnings, so he has used repeated examples, a clear structure and an intense final stanza to make his message as clear as possible.

1 In democratic Western societies, it is often easy to take liberty for granted. Does this poem make you think about this more deeply?

2 Osundare's poem seems to be saying that if people stand up together against their oppressors, they will be stronger. If this is the case, why do you think people so often don't do this?

Author profile

Moniza Alvi was born in Lahore, Pakistan, but left when she was just a few months old and grew up in Hertfordshire. She studied at the universities of York and London. After a long career as a school teacher, she now lives in south-west London with her husband and young daughter. She tutors for the Open College of the Arts and the Poetry School.

Presents from My Aunts in Pakistan

They sent me a salwar kameez
      peacock-blue,
        and another
    glistening like an orange split open,
5 embossed slippers, gold and black
        points curling.
  Candy-striped glass bangles
        snapped, drew blood.
  Like at school, fashions changed
10   in Pakistan –
the salwar bottoms were broad and stiff,
        then narrow.
My aunts chose an apple-green sari,
    silver-bordered
15   for my teens.

I tried each satin-silken top –
    was alien in the sitting-room.
I could never be as lovely
        as those clothes –
20   I longed
for denim and corduroy.
    My costume clung to me
        and I was aflame,
I couldn't rise up out of its fire,
25   half-English,
        unlike Aunt Jamila.

I wanted my parents' camel-skin lamp –
    switching it on in my bedroom,
to consider the cruelty
30   and the transformation
from camel to shade,
    marvel at the colours
        like stained glass.

My mother cherished her jewellery –
35   Indian gold, dangling, filigree.
        But it was stolen from our car.

The presents were radiant in my wardrobe.
    My aunts requested cardigans
        from Marks and Spencers.
40 My salwar kameez
    didn't impress the schoolfriend
who sat on my bed, asked to see
    my weekend clothes.
But often I admired the mirror-work,
45   tried to glimpse myself
        in the miniature
glass circles, recall the story
    how the three of us
        sailed to England.
50 Prickly heat had me screaming on the way.
    I ended up in a cot
in my English grandmother's dining-room,
    found myself alone,
        playing with a tin-boat.

55 I pictured my birthplace
    from fifties' photographs.
        When I was older
there was conflict, a fractured land
    throbbing through newsprint.
60 Sometimes I saw Lahore –
        my aunts in shaded rooms,
screened from male visitors,
    sorting presents,
        wrapping them in tissue.
65 Or there were beggars, sweeper-girls
    and I was there –
        of no fixed nationality,
staring through fretwork
    at the Shalimar Gardens.

Moniza Alvi

Poems from Different Cultures and Traditions   CLUSTER 2

Key Terms

Salwar kameez – traditional dress in India and Pakistan consisting of loose trousers (the salwar) and a loose shirt (the kameez).

Sari – traditional dress in India and Pakistan; it is loose, flowing and often brightly coloured.

Lahore – the second largest city in Pakistan.

Shalimar Gardens – well-known gardens in Lahore.

Making sense of the poem

1 Go through the poem highlighting all of the colours and adjectives used to describe the clothes mentioned in the poem. Put these into a table of Pakistani and English clothes.

2 How would you describe the clothes (the presents of the title) mentioned in the first fifteen lines of the poem?

3 Why do you think Moniza Alvi mentions the bangles snapping and drawing blood (line 8)?

4 How did wearing the clothes in England make the girl feel?

5 How did the girl's schoolfriend respond to her exotic clothes?

6 Despite the reaction of her schoolfriend and her own longing for Western clothing, the presents are important to her. Explain why, using both your own words and lines from the poem.

7 In contrast to the fifteen lines spent describing the clothes from Pakistan, just two lines (20 and 21) are given to the English clothes. What impression does this give of a) the clothes, and b) the speaker's mood?

8 What did the aunts in Pakistan want as presents? What does this show about taste in different communities?

9 What attitude to her parents' past is shown in her desire to own their camel-skin lamp?

10 What images of Pakistan did she have in her youth?

11 How did this change as she grew older? Now look back at your answer to question 6 and see if you can add any other point.

12 What does the girl mean when she says she is of "no fixed nationality" (line 67)?

BACKGROUND

In an interview Moniza Alvi has said: "Growing up I felt that my origins were invisible, because there weren't many people to identify with in Hatfield at that time, of a mixed race background or indeed from any other race, so I felt there was a bit of a blank drawn over that. I think I had a fairly typically English 50s/60s upbringing.

When I eventually went to Pakistan I certainly didn't feel that was home, I'd never felt so English. But I never feel entirely at home in England, and of course I'm not part of the Asian community at all. And it feels a bit odd sometimes that because of the group of poems that I've written about my Asian background, I sometimes tend to be identified as a black writer. I tend to think of England as being very culturally mixed now.

But it's important to know where you come from, which is perhaps what I was lacking as a child. I think it's important to know what has gone into your making, even quite far back, I think it gives you a sense perhaps of richness."

The purpose of the poem

This poem uses clothing as a way of expressing a girl's sense of unease with her identity.

1 With a partner discuss the importance of clothing in expressing your personality as you grow up.

2 Do you sympathise with the girl in the poem? Have your own parents expected you to wear clothing that you found embarrassing?

3 Does any possession you own have especial importance to you because of who gave it to you or because it reminds you of your past?

4 Do you think Moniza Alvi's use of clothing in the poem communicates her ideas effectively?

The poet's approach

The use of verbs in the early part of this poem is interesting:

> They sent
> My aunts chose
> I tried … was alien
> I could never
> I longed
> I was aflame
> I couldn't rise up
> I wanted
> My mother cherished
> My aunts requested.

1   With a partner discuss how the use of verbs highlights the different attitudes of the girl and her aunts.

2   Identify some of the verbs after the "But" in line 44. Do you detect a change in attitude?

At the heart of the poem is an ambivalent relationship with Pakistan. One the one hand the girl feels "alien in the sitting-room" when she tries on her clothes, but on the other she "wanted my parents' camel-skin lamp" and "admired the mirror-work".

3   With a partner discuss the following five lines:

> My costume clung to me
> > and I was aflame,
> I couldn't rise up out of its fire,
> > half-English,
> > > unlike Aunt Jamila.

- Why do you think Moniza Alvi has used the word "clung"? What does it suggest about the girl's attitude to the clothes?

- Why do you think the poet has used the fire metaphor to describe the girl's feelings?

- What do the last two lines of this extract reveal about how the girl feels about herself?

4   What do the details of the aunts' lives at the end of the poem show about life in Pakistan for women?

5   Look at the final four lines of the poem. The poet uses the image of the girl "staring through fretwork". What does this suggest to you about her position? Do you feel that the poet would feel at home in Pakistan? Why?

Gathering your thoughts

This poem explores ideas of belonging but does not suggest any easy answers. The speaker in the poem is fascinated by her origins in Pakistan and embarrassed about them at the same time. She does not feel fully at home in England, nor does she feel fully at home in Pakistan.

1   Do you agree with the conclusion of the poem that the speaker is of "no fixed nationality"? Give your reasons.

2   Is it important for people to feel at home somewhere in the world?

Author profile

Grace Nichols was born in Georgetown, Guyana, in 1950. She worked as a teacher and a journalist, and spent some time in the most remote areas of the country, as part of her degree at the University of Guyana. This period influenced her writing and began a strong interest in Guyanese folk tales. She came to live in Britain at the age of seventeen and now lives in Sussex with her partner, John Agard.

Hurricane Hits England

It took a hurricane, to bring her closer
To the landscape.
Half the night she lay awake,
The howling ship of the wind,
5 Its gathering rage,
Like some dark ancestral spectre.
Fearful and reassuring.

Talk to me Huracan
Talk to me Oya
10 Talk to me Shango
And Hattie,
My sweeping, back-home cousin.

Tell me why you visit
An English coast?
15 What is the meaning
Of old tongues
Reaping havoc
In new places?

The blinding illumination,
20 Even as you short-
Circuit us
Into further darkness?

What is the meaning of trees
Falling heavy as whales
25 Their crusted roots
Their cratered graves?

O why is my heart unchained?

Tropical Oya of the Weather,
I am aligning myself to you,
30 I am following the movement of your winds,
I am riding the mystery of your storm.

Ah, sweet mystery,

Come to break the frozen lake in me,
Shaking the foundations of the very trees within me,
35 Come to let me know
That the earth is the earth is the earth.

Grace Nichols

BACKGROUND

This poem was written after hurricane-force winds hit the southern coast of England in 1987, causing a great deal of damage to houses, trees and electrical supply lines. Hurricanes are common in the Caribbean, where the woman in the poem grew up, but rare in England.

Key Terms

Hurrican – the West Indian god of the wind.

Oya and **Shango** – storm gods, originally of the Yoruba people of Nigeria.

Hattie – the name given to a particularly strong Caribbean hurricane that devastated parts of Belize in October 1961.

Making sense of the poem

1 With a partner read through the poem, then go back and reread stanzas 1, 3, 4 and 5 which most clearly describe the hurricane. Jot down what you understand to be happening and the effect of the hurricane *on the landscape.*

2 Now reread the whole poem, looking for any evidence of the effect of the hurricane *on the woman herself.* What links your answer to question 1 and this question?

3 One indication of the effect of the hurricane on the woman is the questions it causes her to ask. Highlight all of the questions in the poem. How do these suggest her mood?

4 The second stanza contains four "invocations" or calls to gods. How do these invocations help to establish who the speaker is and where she is from?

5 In the fifth stanza the woman asks the storm to explain the meaning of trees being uprooted. What personal message might this have for her?

6 The sixth stanza consists of the single line:

O why is my heart unchained?

What do you think the woman means by this question? Why is the line on its own? How does the poem change after this line?

7 What attitude is being expressed when the woman says that she is aligning herself with Oya of the Weather?

8 What is the message of the hurricane?

The purpose of the poem

1 With a partner discuss the opening two lines of the poem. What do they imply about the strength of the woman's connections to her home?

Hurricanes are destructive forces that cause disorder and chaos. For the poet, though, the hurricane has an altogether different effect because out of the disorder comes peace and understanding.

2 Write a few sentences explaining in your own words the purpose of the poem.

The poet's approach

STRUCTURE

The poem shifts around in its approach as the woman responds to the storm. After an introductory stanza in the third person, the gods are first invoked and then questioned. They do not answer, but the speaker feels released by asking the questions and then comes to a new understanding of her situation.

1 **Copy out and fill in the following table to identify the techniques used and the purpose of each section.**

Section	Technique	Purpose
Stanza 1	Third-person description	Introduces the woman and her distance from the English landscape
Stanza 2		
Stanzas 3–5		
Stanza 6		
Stanzas 7–8		

LANGUAGE

The first stanza does a great deal of work and is worth looking at in detail. The first three lines introduce the woman and her situation. We are then told of the:

> ... howling ship of the wind.

This powerful metaphor, perhaps suggesting a sailing ship, with the wind tearing through its rigging, moving violently in a storm, is made even more powerful when the wind is said to be:

> Like some dark ancestral spectre.

Now the ship of the wind is a sort of ghost ship, like the *Flying Dutchman*, forever tossed by storms. All of the images in this part of the poem give a sense of power and strength, even destructiveness (as when we learn of the wind's "gathering rage"). The last line of the stanza, therefore, is rather surprising:

> Fearful and reassuring.

The idea of a storm being reassuring makes more sense when you have read the whole poem, but at this point it is completely unexpected.

In stanza 3 the woman asks the question:

> What is the meaning
> Of old tongues
> Reaping havoc
> In new places?

1 Explain as fully as you can how "old tongues" can cause "havoc". What part of the storm is she referring to here?

2 "Blinding illumination" (line 19) is an example of an oxymoron; that is, a combination of two apparent opposites. Explain the effect Grace Nichols is trying to achieve with this phrase. Could the word "illumination" have a further meaning?

3 What is happening to the woman when she says that the frozen lake in her is being broken and that the roots of the trees within her are being disturbed?

4 Comment on Grace Nichol's use of metaphors and similes in the rest of the poem. Why have they been used? How effective are they?

The poem has an irregular stanza structure but it makes frequent use of repetition, for instance, "Talk to me" is used three times to invoke the gods of the wind.

5 Find other examples of repetition in the poem. How do they help to hold the poem together?

6 Why do you think Grace Nichols has used repetition in the last line?

Gathering your thoughts

The poem uses a rather surprising aspect of the woman's home background to make the unfamiliar familiar. The hurricane disrupts her life in England but it also shakes up her attitude to a place where she had not really felt comfortable.

1 Do you think the storm is a good way of expressing the force for change in the woman's life?

2 A destructive force is here seen as ultimately a force for good in the woman's life. Could the hurricane be used as a metaphor to describe other people's situations or difficult experiences? Give examples.

that will help you choose which poems to group together in your answers.
will find the examiner's mark scheme for the mock questions.

Grouping the poems by subject matter and theme

	People	Place	Culture/ tradition	History/ change	Description	Identity/ language	Politics
Cluster 1							
Limbo			✓	✓		✓	
Nothing's Changed		✓	✓	✓	✓	✓	✓
Island Man	✓	✓	✓				
Blessing		✓	✓		✓		
Two Scavengers	✓	✓	✓				✓
Night of the Scorpion	✓		✓				
Vultures		✓					✓
What Were They Like?		✓	✓	✓			✓
Cluster 2							
from Search for My Tongue	✓		✓			✓	
from Unrelated Incidents			✓			✓	✓
Half-caste	✓		✓			✓	✓
Love after Love	✓	✓		✓		✓	
This Room	✓	✓	✓		✓	✓	
Not My Business	✓	✓					✓
Presents from My Aunt in Pakistan	✓	✓	✓			✓	
Hurricane Hits England	✓	✓	✓		✓	✓	

Getting a Grade C

MOCK QUESTION 1

What do you think is important to two of the poets that you have studied about the culture or cultures they are writing about?

Write about:

- what you have learned from the poems about the cultures
- what you think is important to each poet
- how the language helps to bring out the cultures
- your own response to the poem.

Planning and structuring your response

It is vital that you plan your essay before you begin writing. In this way, you will ensure that you have a focused and well-structured argument, rather than a series of unconnected points.

When answering the question, it's important to look at the ways in which the poets express their ideas about the cultures they are writing about. Most people find writing about the content of a poem relatively easy, so it is the more difficult examination of the poet's techniques that is rewarded with the best grades.

The grid below should help you to think about what you need to focus on if you choose "Hurricane Hits England" and "Not My Business". Copy the grid and fill it in, adding to it if necessary. Construct your own grid if you choose different poems.

What	How	Evidence
Hurricane Hits England		
Poet did not feel at home in England	Implied by opening statement	"It took a hurricane, to bring her closer to the landscape"
A sense of where you come from is important for the poet's identity	References to the gods, and to the slave ships	
Poet had turned her back on the Caribbean	Imagery	Her heart is "unchained" by the hurricane, and the "frozen lake" inside her is broken
Poet retains her Caribbean identity, even though she lives in England	Statement at end	

What	How	Evidence
Not My Business		
African setting	Names and other references	
The political regime (probably in Nigeria) is brutal and corrupt	Narrative: four people are abducted and assaulted by soldiers for no apparent reason	
Narrator shows the wrong attitude	Use of refrain	"What business of mine is it/So long they don't take the yam/From my savouring mouth"

Analysing sample responses

Below are the first paragraphs of two responses to this question. The first is a grade D and the second is a grade C. Show why the essays have been awarded these grades by indicating where they fulfil the examiner's assessment criteria (see page 32). One example has been given in each case. How could you turn the grade D extract into a grade C?

1

I am going to discuss the way that Grace Nichols and Niyi Osundare present culture in their poems "Hurricane Hits England" and "Not My Business". I intend to look at what is important to the poets about the cultures and what they are trying to say about them, from the language they use to describe them.

Grace Nichols's poem "Hurricane Hits England" is about just that, but it is what the storm means to the poet that what really matters. As hurricanes in England aren't normal, the poet is surprised by it and it reminds her of the Caribbean where they are more common. In a strange way, the hurricane makes her feel at home. She feels that the hurricane is speaking to her and freeing her from the feeling that she does not really belong in England but wonders why her heart has been "unchained" by such an event. Niyi Osundare seems to be talking about the what can happen if there's a culture where people only take care of themselves. In the first three stanzas, there are stories of three people who are in some way attacked by the state without the reader knowing why. The speaker in the poem does not care because nothing has happened to him and "they" haven't taken the food from his "savouring mouth". In the fourth stanza though, things change for the speaker. From the names of the people in the poem, you can tell that this is set in Africa and the speaker mentions "yams" which are a West African fruit.

awareness of feeling(s), attitudes(s), and ideas

In this essay, I shall discuss how culture is presented in "Not My Business" and "Hurricane Hits England". Grace Nichols's poem tells us about her feelings as to both English and Caribbean culture while Niyi Osunadare writes about the climate of fear that can exist in military dictatorships. In this case, he is writing about Nigeria.

"Hurricane Hits England" is a very personal poem in which Nichols writes of how "It took a hurricane to bring her closer to the landscape". By this she means that she did not feel at home in England until the hurricane arrived as they are something that she would normally associate with the Caribbean. She sees the winds as having been sent by African gods (where many of the Caribbean population first came from) and feels that they have come to let her know "That the earth is the earth is the earth". By this she is saying that although you may feel at home in a particular climate, there is no reason why you should not make your home anywhere. Grace Nichols's poem is talking about culture in a very different way to Niyi Osundare, who is interested in a society where people are afraid they may be "dragged...off to a lengthy absence" for no reason.

awareness of authorial techniques and purpose

Over to you ...

Now answer the question yourself, with your own choice of poems, bearing in mind the things you need to do to score a grade C. Make sure that you spend no longer than 45 minutes on it.

EXAM SKILLS FOCUS – Saying something new

When making statements about poems it is important to ensure that you are saying something new about it rather than simply re-stating what is in the poem in different words.

Here are some statements about "Not My Business". Which ones say something new, and which simply re-state what is in the poem?

- The poet says that Akanni was beaten up and taken away, while Chinwe turned up to work to discover that her job had disappeared.
- The poet says that the state has a number of different ways of intimidating and victimising people but it doesn't seem to care who it picks.
- The speaker in the poem does not seem to mind what happens to other people provided that he gets his food at the end of the day.
- Food is obviously a very important commodity in poor countries and the threat of hunger is a powerful weapon for the oppressors.

The new information will generally be your **opinion** and this must be backed up with evidence.

See the Exam Skills Focus on page 78.

Getting a Grade C

> ## Mock Question 2
>
> **Write about description in any two poems.**
>
> Write about:
>
> - what is described
> - how it is described
> - ideas that are brought out by the description
> - what the descriptions make you think and feel.

Planning and structuring your response

Before tackling the question, it is important to decide on the points you want to make and the order you wish to present them. The most important thing to bring out is the effects the descriptions have on the reader and the way the poets achieve these effects. This will score more highly than simply describing what is in each poem.

The grid below will help you think about what you need to focus on if you choose "Presents from my Aunts" and "Half-caste". Copy it out and fill it in, adding to it if necessary. Construct your own grid if you choose different poems.

What	How	Evidence
Presents from My Aunts in Pakistan		
Description of the clothes sent from Pakistan	Detailed description – some use of metaphor and simile	"like an orange split open"
Speaker doesn't feel comfortable wearing them	Metaphor	
Yet she is fascinated with the clothes	Contrast between the elaborate Pakistani clothes and the dull Western clothes	Simply "denim and corduroy"
Description at end implies she is cut off from both cultures	Symbolism	"Staring through fretwork at the Shalimar Gardens"
Half-caste		
"Half-caste" is ridiculed as a term	Irony – using term to describe great art and music	
Ironic idea of things being half present	Repetition	"half-a-hand", "half-a-eye", "half-a-dream", "half-a-shadow"
Humour in the description	Puns	"caste/overcast"

Analysing a sample response

With a partner read the opening paragraphs of the essay below and decide on the grade you would award it. Make sure that you can back up what you say with reference to the assessment criteria on page 32.

Both "Presents from my Aunts in Pakistan" and "Half-Caste" make very effective use of description but and although the poems are in many ways very different, they are both concerned with being stuck between two cultures and not being really accepted by either.

Moniza Alvi's poem begins by describing the clothes that are sent to her by her aunts in Pakistan. The clothes all seem to be very bright and colourful but the poet does not seem to want to wear them outside. This might be because she doesn't want to be seen outside by her school friends in an "apple green sari" and it might be because she would rather wear jeans and cords. "Half-Caste" is a very different poem that is not written in standard English but talks about the way in which it is silly to view people who are of mixed race as different. He describes how it's stupid to see anything as "half-caste" and asks if Picasso's paintings are "half-caste" because they mix colours or Tchaichovsky's music is because it mixes "notes".

"Presents from my Aunts in Pakistan" also describes the poet's experiences of her journey to England as well as how she imagines Pakistan to be from photographs she has seen. Both the memory of the journey and the way she imagines Pakistan are vague. She can't remember much of the journey and only recalls playing in her grandmother's dining room. Her ideas of Pakistan are made up from "fifties photographs" and things she has heard. This is a good way of showing that she doesn't feel she really belongs in the culture. John Agard, however, is really against judging people as if they don't belong and gives an example by describing the British weather as nearly always half-caste because it is so often a mixture of cloud and sky.

When you have decided on the grade you would award this extract, make a list of its strengths and weaknesses. What needs to be improved?

Over to you ...

Now tackle the question on your own, with your own choice of poems, ensuring that you spend no longer than 45 minutes on it.

The Exam Skills Focus section on page 78 and at other points in this book will help you with your response.

EXAM SKILLS FOCUS – Gathering evidence

When gathering evidence the key question is: How do you know that?

In an ordinary conversation, when two people are discussing a poem for instance, the answer might seem obvious, but when writing in an exam it is essential that you **show exactly how you arrived at a particular observation or conclusion.**

This means that:

- if you mention the poet's use of a metaphor, you should quote it
- if you state that the poem has a personal point of view, you need to explain how you determined this
- if you say that the poem has a sad or comic tone, you should refer to or quote the parts of the poem that lead you to this conclusion
- if you decide that the theme of the poem is "solitude", you need to gather together all the parts of the poem that lead you to your opinion.

Go back to the essay you have just written. For each statement that you made, refer to or quote the evidence to back it up.

Getting a Grade A

MOCK QUESTION 1

Compare the ways in which two poems from this selection explore the idea that your identity is closely linked with the language you use.

Planning and structuring your response

Before starting to write, it's important to plan your answer, working out the order of what you want to say. The two most obvious poems to compare would be the extracts from "Search for My Tongue" and "Unrelated Incidents", as they are the two poems that deal most clearly with languages and their cultural implications.

The grid below will help you think about what you need to focus on in these poems. Copy the grid and fill it in, adding to it if necessary. Construct your own grid if you choose different poems.

What	How	Evidence
From "Search for My Tongue"		
Poet uses tongue to mean both organ and language	Extended metaphor	
Loss of identity is terrible	Powerful imagery	"Your mother tongue would rot"
The return of the mother tongue is like the return of life itself	Extended metaphor (lines 31–38)	
from "Unrelated Incidents"		
Poem explores the way class and education are judged according to how people speak	Use of non-standard English	
Poet is annoyed that people are judged by their accents	Implied	"yi widny wahnt/mi ti talk/aboot thi/truth wia/voice lik/wanna yoo/scruff"
Poet ridicules BBC accents	Irony – the newsreader actually speaks in a thick Glaswegian accent	

Analysing sample responses

Read the extracts below from two responses to this question. The first is a grade B response and the second is a grade A. Show why the essays have been awarded these grades by indicating where they fulfil the examiner's assessment criteria (see page 32). One example has been given in each case. How could you turn the B extract into a grade A?

1

In "Search for My Tongue", Sujata Bhatt writes about the problem many bi-lingual people might face when they live away from the country where they grew up. The poet seem to be worried that she will forget her first language because she never speaks it. She sees language as more than just a simple means of communicating with people because it represents her original culture as well. You can tell that she is worried that she will forget the language and sees this as an entirely negative thing by the words that she uses. The idea that: "your mother tongue would rot, rot and die in your mouth" is an unpleasant image because having something rotting in your mouth would be physically sickening.

The extended metaphor in the last eight lines of the poem is in direct contrast to the ideas of sickness and decay. Bhatt likens Gujerati to a plant growing stronger until "it pushes the other tongue aside" and "blossoms out of my mouth". The poet clearly finds the experience of dreaming in Gujerati a reassuring one as it shows her that she has not lost touch with where she comes from.

Tom Leonard also writes about language but in a different way. Like Bhatt, he sees the way people speak as a way of telling which culture people come from but he does not like the way that people assume things about the class and intelligence of the speaker from the accent they use. He seems angry that the people who speak with a strong accent would not be newsreaders because people would not take them seriously, as though things that are important and reliable news can only be given in a "BBC accent". He is angry that people think "thirza right way ti spell ana right way ti tok it".

understanding of a variety of writer's techniques

2

In "Search for My Tongue" Sujata Bhatt uses two meanings of the word "tongue" –both "language" and "the physical organ in the mouth". This double meaning is at the crux of the poem as her "mother tongue" becomes a part of the body and to lose it is seen as far more significant for the poet than simply forgetting information that she no longer has any use for. A person's mother tongue will provide the basis of their cultural background as languages evolve around cultures. Forms of expression will grow up around the way of life in a country – hence the fact that there are some words *in every language that are very difficult to translate into another. Perhaps this is why Bhatt writes that:*

> *You could not use them both together*
> *Even If you thought that way.*

To lose your mother tongue would therefore be to lose a sense of where you come from as well as your original cultural identity. Bhatt underlines how upsetting she finds this prospect through the idea that her tongue would "rot and die in her mouth". This notion of decay and death contrasts very strongly with spring-like healthy images in her dream where the language "blossoms out of my mouth".

analysis of a variety of
writer's techniques

Over to you ...

Now tackle the question on your own, with your own choice of poems, ensuring that you spend no longer than 45 minutes on it.

The Exam Skills Focus below and at other points in the book will help you to do this.

EXAM SKILLS FOCUS – Using quotations and examples

You will not have much time in this exam so it is important not to waste it by copying out quotations unnecessarily. You need to make sure that your examples are relevant to your answer as a whole and support the point you are making. There are three main ways of supporting your views:

- **The reference.** This is where you talk about the poem without quoting it directly:

  John Agard uses three examples to illustrate the advantages of mixing, involving painting, the English weather and music.

- **The embedded quotation.** Embedded quotations are usually short and are enclosed in inverted commas. You do not need to start a new line:

  Tom Leonard uses a number of non standard spellings, such as "wanna you scruff" and "yi canny talk right", to give an impression of a speaker with a strong accent.

- **Full-line quotations.** Full-line quotations do not use quotation marks and should be set out exactly as they are on the page. They should be used sparingly and generally when a point is being made about such things as rhyming, end-stopped lines or layout:

  The slight pause between the two occurrences of the word "rot" makes the idea stand out even more:

  > *your mother tongue would rot*
  > *rot and die in your mouth*

Getting a Grade A

MOCK QUESTION 2

Write about the ways in which two poets in this selection explore the connection between people and the places in which they live.

PLANNING AND STRUCTURING YOUR RESPONSE

Before starting to write, it's important to plan your answer, working out the order of what you want to say. There are several poems in the anthology exploring people's connections with the places in which they live. The places and everything to do with them – weather, landscape, other people – provide important details about the background of the poems and the culture they describe.

The grid below will help you think about what you need to focus on if you choose "This Room" and "Love After Love". Copy the grid and fill it in, adding to it if necessary. Construct your own grid if you choose different poems.

What	How	Evidence
This Room		
The speaker seems to live in one room, suggesting poverty	Implied in description	It contains both "the bed" and the "pots and pans"
Poem presents the room as oppressive	Use of language	
The mood of the speaker is projected onto the place in which she lives	Personification	"Pots and pans bang together/in celebration"
Set in a hot country (probably Asian)	Implied in description	
Love After Love		
Sense of ownership underlines the idea of relaxing in own space	Repetition	"At your own door, in your own mirror"
It is a place where you can nurture yourself	Imagery of feasting	
You have been there for years	Implied in description	"love letters", "photographs" and "desperate notes" have all been collected and stored in the bookshelf

Analysing a sample response

With a partner, read the opening paragraphs of the essay below and decide on the grade you would award it. Make sure that you back up what you say with reference to the assessment criteria on page 32.

The connection between people and the places in which they live is explored in both "Love After Love" by Derek Walcott and "This Room" by Imtiaz Dharker. Although both poems explore the way people feel more than the places they are set in, the settings are important to the overall effects of the poems.

In "Love After Love", the speaker in the poem has been in the place he lives for a long time and he is at home there. You can tell this because he mentions that you will meet yourself "at your own door" and "in your own mirror". The fact that he uses the word "own" twice makes it clear that the person is very familiar with the surroundings. In the second stanza, there is reference to the giving of food and drink and in the last stanza there is the image of feasting "on your life". Once again, the atmosphere seems to be one of comfort.

In stanzas three and four, there is also the idea of taking down the "love letters", the "photographs" and "the desperate notes" from "the bookshelf". The collection of all of these things in one place seems to suggest that that they have been put there over a period of years, as though the speaker is collecting his past into a comfortable hoard. Although the poet talks of greeting "yourself", the overall message of the poem seems to be to make yourself comfortable and enjoy the memories.

"This Room" by Imtiaz Dharker is in some ways a similar poem in that both deal with ideas that are physically impossible. The poem seems to show a change from misery to happiness. The room itself and the things in the room are seen as a part of the experience, perhaps because they have been there when the speaker in the poem was unhappy. Therefore, when the speaker's mood changes, it is as though "the bed is lifting out of its nightmares". When the speaker mentions that the "improbable arrives", suggesting that something good has happened that she was not expecting, "the pots and pans bang together in celebration". In other words, the happiness felt is shown metaphorically through the objects in the room which seem to join in the celebration. Unlike Walcott's poem which suggests quiet, comfortable and measured contemplation, "This Room" is about a sudden sense of joy which allows the speaker to forget that she lives in just one room.

When you have decided on the grade you would award this extract, make a list of its strengths and weaknesses. What needs to be improved?

Over to you ...

Now tackle the question on your own, with your own choice of poems, ensuring that you spend no longer than 45 minutes on it.

The Exam Skills Focus section found below and at other points in this book will help you with your response.

EXAM SKILLS FOCUS – The writer's techniques

"Understanding of a variety of writer's techniques" will earn you a B grade, while "analysis of a variety of writer's techniques" will get you an A. At first it may not seem as though there is much difference between the two criteria.

1 Discuss with a partner what you think the difference is between "understanding" and "analysis" of a writer's techniques.

2 Look closely at the examples below and decide which of the statements demonstrate understanding and which demonstrate analysis.

(a) The bed "lifting out of its nightmares" uses personification to demonstrate the movement from bad to good in the poem as it is a good thing for even a bed to wake up out of a nightmare.

(b) The bed "lifting out of its nightmares" is another example of the objects in the room being used to express emotions. Normally we would expect the person in the bed to be rising to a more pleasant time, but by saying here that the bed itself had nightmares Imtiaz Dharker implies that nightmares are a frequent part of normal existence in the room.

(c) The phrase "off to a lengthy absence" is quite striking. It is literally impossible to go off on an absence, or if not impossible, very disturbing. Where would someone on an "absence" actually be? The phrase also has echoes of such things as "a lengthy illness" or a "lengthy silence" as opposed to "a long holiday" or "a long rest".

(d) The first three verses of "Not my Business" end in a chorus. These sum up the attitude of the speaker who is only interested in his own business and his food. The last verse has no chorus because the speaker of the poem, who said it, is no longer there.

English Literature: Poetry

Author profile

Seamus Heaney was born into a Roman Catholic farming family in Northern Ireland in 1939. His poetry often concerns rural life, how people change as they mature, and death. Heaney searched for a way to relate thoughts and feelings about political events in Northern Ireland without becoming propagandist. He has published many poetry collections and, in 1995, was awarded the Nobel Prize for literature.

Storm on the Island

We are prepared: we build our houses squat,
Sink walls in rock and roof them with good slate.
The wizened earth has never troubled us
With hay, so, as you can see, there are no stacks
5 Or stooks that can be lost. Nor are there trees
Which might prove company when it blows full
Blast: you know what I mean – leaves and branches
Can raise a tragic chorus in a gale
So that you can listen to the thing you fear
10 Forgetting that it pummels your house too.
But there are no trees, no natural shelter.
You might think that the sea is company,
Exploding comfortably down on the cliffs
But no: when it begins, the flung spray hits
15 The very windows, spits like a tame cat
Turned savage. We just sit tight while wind dives
And strafes invisibly. Space is a salvo.
We are bombarded by the empty air.
Strange, it is a huge nothing that we fear.

Reading for meaning

1 What do the islanders' preparations for the storm imply about its expected strength?

2 What picture of the island is given by the things that the islanders do *not* have to worry about?

3 How might the sound of wind in the trees be a distraction in a storm? What are the islanders most concerned about?

4 How might the sea provide company?

5 How does the sea actually affect the islanders in the storm?

6 What is strange about the thing that the islanders fear?

Literary techniques

1 What is the tone of the opening sentence of the poem? How does this change as the poem progresses?

2 How would you describe the attitude expressed in the words "The wizened earth has never troubled us/With hay"?

3 Why do you think Heaney shifts from "we" to "I" when discussing the wind in the trees? Why does he also address the reader as "you" at this point?

4 What is interesting about Heaney's use of the words "exploding comfortably"?

5 What is the normal attitude of the islander to the sea, conveyed through the simile "spits like a tame cat/Turned savage"?

6 What attitude to the storm is conveyed through Heaney's use of words such as "dives and strafes", "salvo" and "bombarded"?

7 In what sense is a storm a "huge nothing"? What technical term is applied to this kind of phrase? Why has the poet used this technique?

Themes

"Storm on the Island" is unusual for Heaney in that it is not written from a personal point of view. It has a more general aim, describing life in rural Ireland and pointing out the harshness of existence in the countryside. The main purpose of the poem is to express the power of the elements of air and water on people wedded to the earth.

The Perch

Perch on their water-perch hung in the clear Bann River
Near the clay bank in alder-dapple and waver,

Perch we called 'grunts', little flood-slubs, runty and ready,
I saw and I see in the river's glorified body

5 That is passable through, but they're bluntly holding the pass,
Under the water-roof, over the bottom, adoze,

Guzzling the current, against it, all muscle and slur
In the finland of perch, the fenland of alder, on air

That is water, on carpets of Bann stream, on hold
10 In the everything flows and steady go of the world.

Reading for meaning

1 What position in the water is suggested by the term "water-perch"?

2 Which tree is above the bank at this point in the river?

3 Are the perch that Heaney is observing fully grown?

4 Where in the river have the perch positioned themselves?

5 Do the perch seem particularly alert?

6 What do the perch have to do to stay still?

7 What does Heaney find interesting about the stillness of the perch?

Literary techniques

1 What do the terms "water-perch", "water-roof" and "air/That is water" suggest about how Heaney sees the perch?

2 The poem is noticeable for its use of sound. Words often echo or repeat an earlier sound so that that there is a smooth flow of sound throughout the poem. Find examples of this echoing throughout the poem and comment on their effect.

3 Why do you think Heaney has chosen his words in this way?

4 Two of the words in this poem are not in standard dictionaries – "slubs" and "adoze".

   • Suggest a meaning for "slubs". What other words does it remind you of?

   • Suggest a meaning for "adoze". Why is it is better than "asleep" or "dozing"?

5 The phrase "holding the pass" refers to soldiers using a narrow place to hold off an enemy. In what way are the perch like soldiers?

6 "Guzzling the current" is a transferred epithet, as the perch are actually guzzling things *in* the current. Why do you think Heaney has used this phrase here?

7 One of the meanings of "slur" is to run notes together. Why is this is a good choice of word at this point?

8 In the fourth stanza Heaney puns on "finland". How does this image help to expand the world of the river?

9 The final description of the perch, "on hold/In the everything flows and steady go of the world", suggests that there is something special about the perch's immobility. How is this expressed in the sound and rhythm of these lines?

Themes

This poem seems to be describing the stillness and tranquillity of the perch, but their lack of movement and apparent sleepiness is the result of a hard won struggle against the prevailing current. Heaney seems to imply that any kind of tranquillity needs to wrestled from the prevailing flow "and steady go of the world."

Although there are no obvious autobiographical links in this poem, it is definitely based on the poet's personal experience. Seamus Heaney has said that: "quite often the kind of poem I write is just an attempt to get back", and that "these perch, although they are actually in the river, they are very much in a kind of 55 year old memory lake of my own".

Blackberry-Picking

for Philip Hobsbaum

Late August, given heavy rain and sun
For a full week, the blackberries would ripen.
At first, just one, a glossy purple clot
Among others, red, green, hard as a knot.
5 You ate that first one and its flesh was sweet
Like thickened wine: summer's blood was in it
Leaving stains upon the tongue and lust for
Picking. Then red ones inked up and that hunger
Sent us out with milk-cans, pea-tins, jam-pots
10 Where briars scratched and wet grass bleached our boots.
Round hayfields, cornfields and potato-drills
We trekked and picked until the cans were full,
Until the tinkling bottom had been covered
With green ones, and on top big dark blobs burned
15 Like a plate of eyes. Our hands were peppered
With thorn pricks, our palms sticky as Bluebeard's.

We hoarded the fresh berries in the byre.
But when the bath was filled we found a fur,
A rat-grey fungus, glutting on our cache.
20 The juice was stinking too. Once off the bush
The fruit fermented, the sweet flesh would turn sour.
I always felt like crying. It wasn't fair
That all the lovely canfuls smelt of rot.
Each year I hoped they'd keep, knew they would not.

Reading for meaning

1 How do unripe blackberries look and feel?

2 What was special about the taste of the first ripe blackberry?

3 What was the effect of tasting it?

4 What are the problems associated with blackberry-picking?

5 What did the pickers do with their treasures?

6 What happened to the picked blackberries?

Literary techniques

1 In the first stanza Heaney uses a number of images that associate blackberries and their juice with flesh and blood. What image from horror films is suggested by the lines below?

  • its flesh was sweet

  • Like thickened wine: summer's blood was in it

  • Leaving stains upon the tongue and lust for/picking.

2 What other image from children's stories also suggests a link between the blackberry juice and blood?

3 What is suggested by the idea of a "plate of eyes"?

4 The first stanza also expresses the enthusiasm of the blackberry-pickers for their task. What techniques does Heaney use to show this enthusiasm?

5 What is suggested by the alliteration on the "f" and "s" sounds in stanza 2?

6 The poem mostly uses half rhymes. Identify the two places in the poem that use full rhymes and explain why you think Heaney has used them at these points.

7 What point of view is suggested by the phrase "It wasn't fair"?

8 What point of view is suggested by the last line of the poem?

Themes

This poem uses a childhood reminiscence to reflect on the difficulty of making good things last. The joy and enthusiasm of the first stanza is balanced by the disappointment and frustration of the second. Although the mood of the first stanza is light-hearted, the association of the blackberries with blood suggests that the fate of the blackberries is common to all life. The final two lines express a hard-won adult perspective.

Death of a Naturalist

All year the flax-dam festered in the heart
Of the townland; green and heavy headed
Flax had rotted there, weighted down by huge sods.
Daily it sweltered in the punishing sun.
5 Bubbles gargled delicately, bluebottles
Wove a strong gauze of sound around the smell.
There were dragon-flies, spotted butterflies,
But best of all was the warm thick slobber
Of frogspawn that grew like clotted water
10 In the shade of the banks. Here, every spring
I would fill jampotfuls of the jellied
Specks to range on window-sills at home,
On shelves at school, and wait and watch until
The fattening dots burst into nimble-
15 Swimming tadpoles. Miss Walls would tell us how
The daddy frog was called a bullfrog
And how he croaked and how the mammy frog
Laid hundreds of little eggs and this was
Frogspawn. You could tell the weather by frogs too
20 For they were yellow in the sun and brown
In rain.

Then one hot day when fields were rank
With cowdung in the grass the angry frogs
Invaded the flax-dam; I ducked through hedges
25 To a coarse croaking that I had not heard
Before. The air was thick with a bass chorus.
Right down the dam gross-bellied frogs were cocked
On sods; their loose necks pulsed like sails. Some hopped:
The slap and plop were obscene threats. Some sat
30 Poised like mud grenades, their blunt heads farting.
I sickened, turned, and ran. The great slime kings
Were gathered there for vengeance and I knew
That if I dipped my hand the spawn would clutch it.

Reading for meaning

1 This poem falls into three sections: lines 1 to 7; lines 8 to 21; and 22 to the end. Give each section a heading that summarises its content.

2 What impression do you get of the flax-dam in the first four lines of the poem?

3 What sort on animal life inhabited the dam?

4 What did the young Heaney do with the frogspawn he collected?

5 What did he learn about frogs at school?

6 How did Heaney feel when he met the frogs at the flax-dam?

7 Why did he suddenly not want to touch the frogspawn?

8 Explain as fully as you can the change in attitude that the poem describes.

Literary techniques

The opening section of the poem is a vivid description of the flax-dam, but Heaney's choice of words and his use of poetic techniques adds an emotional tone to the description.

1 Comment on Heaney's use of the following words and phrases. What overall impression is the poet trying to acheive?

- flax-dam festered
- green and heavy headed
- sweltered in the punishing sun
- bubbles gargled delicately
- bluebottles/wove a strong gauze of sound around the smell.

2 How does the tone change when Heaney begins describing the frogspawn?

3 How does Heaney create a sense of anticipation about the appearance of the tadpoles in lines 13 to 15?

4 What further mood change is signalled by Heaney's description of the fields as being "rank with cowdung"?

5 Find all the words that have a military association in the last section. What does Heaney's use of these terms tell you about his feelings about the frogs?

6 What effect is gained by the use of "slap and plop" to describe the movement of the frogs?

7 How does Heaney use bodily functions to express his sense of disgust?

8 Why do you think Heaney refers to the frogs as "the great slime kings" at the end of the poem? How does this reference compare with the language he uses about them at the end of the first stanza?

Themes

In this autobiographical poem Heaney records a change in his attitude to nature. As a thoughtless boy he had been happy to collect frogspawn, but in the final section of the poem his understanding of its significance in the reproductive cycle of nature causes him disgust and fear.

Digging

Between my finger and my thumb
The squat pen rests; snug as a gun.

Under my window, a clean rasping sound
When the spade sinks into gravelly ground:
5 My father, digging. I look down

Till his straining rump among the flowerbeds
Bends low, comes up twenty years away
Stooping in rhythm through potato drills
Where he was digging.

10 The coarse boot nestled on the lug, the shaft
Against the inside knee was levered firmly.
He rooted out tall tops, buried the bright edge deep
To scatter new potatoes that we picked,
Loving their cool hardness in our hands.

15 By God, the old man could handle a spade.
Just like his old man.

My grandfather cut more turf in a day
Than any other man on Toner's bog.
Once I carried him milk in a bottle
20 Corked sloppily with paper. He straightened up
To drink it, then fell to right away

Nicking and slicing neatly, heaving sods
Over his shoulder, going down and down
For the good turf. Digging.

25 The cold smell of potato mould, the squelch and slap
Of soggy peat, the curt cuts of an edge
Through living roots awaken in my head.
But I've no spade to follow men like them.

Between my finger and my thumb
30 The squat pen rests.
I'll dig with it.

Reading for meaning

In this this deceptively simple poem Heaney recalls the achievements of his father and grandfather and decides on his own future.

1 Where is the writer at the start of the poem?

2 What does the sight of his father digging in the flower bed remind him of?

3 Who else does the writer associate with skill at digging?

4 What memory is he associated with?

5 What skill does the writer decide to use?

Literary techniques

1 The poem makes use of onomatopoeia (words that sound like the noise or action they describe, e.g. *hiss*) in a number of its descriptions. Find and comment on three examples.

2 Why do you think sound is so important in this poem?

3 How does Heaney emphasise the skill and precision of his father's digging?

4 In communicating the skills of his father and grandfather, why do you think Heaney uses particular memories rather than general statements?

5 What does Heaney mean when he says he has "no spade to follow men like them"?

6 In what way does Heaney intend to dig with his pen?

Themes

Heaney was born and brought up in a farming community and in this poem he shows a great deal of respect for the skills, strength and endurance of previous generations. However, he recognises that he does not have the same skills and temperament as his father and grandfather and that it is necessary for him to deploy the talent that he does have. This talent is his ability to write. By writing about his ancestors he is able to make his own contribution to their achievements.

Mid-Term Break

I sat all morning in the college sick bay
Counting bells knelling classes to a close.
At two o'clock our neighbours drove me home.

In the porch I met my father crying –
5 He had always taken funerals in his stride –
And Big Jim Evans saying it was a hard blow.

The baby cooed and laughed and rocked the pram
When I came in, and I was embarrassed
By old men standing up to shake my hand

10 And tell me they were "sorry for my trouble";
Whispers informed strangers that I was the eldest,
Away at school, as my mother held my hand

In hers and coughed out angry tearless sighs.
At ten o'clock the ambulance arrived
15 With the corpse, stanched and bandaged by the nurses.

Next morning I went up into the room. Snowdrops
And candles soothed the bedside; I saw him
For the first time in six weeks. Paler now,

Wearing a poppy bruise on his left temple,
20 He lay in the four foot box as in his cot.
No gaudy scars, the bumper knocked him clear.

A four foot box, a foot for every year.

Reading for meaning

"Mid-Term Break" is an autobiographical account of the death of Seamus Heaney's brother Christopher in a car accident.

1 What is the usual meaning of the phrase "mid-term break"? Suggest two other meanings for the phrase in the context of the poem.

2 Why are neighbours and comparative strangers able to offer comfort to Heaney rather than his mother and father?

3 Why do you think Heaney mentions the response of the baby?

4 What are the dominant colours in the brother's room? How might these be soothing?

5 Why does Heaney compare the coffin to a cot?

6 What does the last line add to our knowledge of Heaney's brother? Why do you think this information is kept until the end?

Literary techniques

The poem describes a journey from a school sick bay to the bedside of Heaney's dead brother.

1 How is the sound of bells used to establish the mood of the poem in the first stanza?

2 How would you describe the mood as Heaney returns home?

3 What mood prevails in the brother's room? How is the mood established. Refer to words and phrases in the poem in your answer.

4 Heaney often makes careful use of sound in his poems. What is the effect on the pace the poem of the internal rhymes and alliteration in line 2?

5 Why do you think Heaney uses so many harsh "a" sounds to describe the arrival of his brother's body in the fifth stanza?

6 Comment on Heaney's use of monosyllables, alliteration and assonance in line 20.

7 None of Seamus Heaney's family say anything in the poem. Big Jim Evans makes an unfortunate pun and the neighbours either whisper gossip or use the conventional phrase "sorry for your trouble". What does this suggest about the power of language in the face of tragedy?

8 Why do you think there are no verbs in the last sentence of the poem?

Themes

In this poem Heaney records what he sees and hears virtually without comment. The only personal emotion he describes is embarrassment at having strangers shake his hand. The emotions of Heaney's parents at the loss of their four-year-old son stand out strongly against this reticence, but so too does the cheerful demeanour of the baby. The death of a brother is deeply sad but it is also part of life and life goes on.

Follower

My father worked with a horse-plough,
His shoulders globed like a full sail strung
Between the shafts and the furrow.
The horse strained at his clicking tongue.

5 An expert. He would set the wing
And fit the bright steel-pointed sock.
The sod rolled over without breaking.
At the headrig, with a single pluck

Of reins, the sweating team turned round
10 And back into the land. His eye
Narrowed and angled at the ground,
Mapping the furrow exactly.

I stumbled in his hob-nailed wake,
Fell sometimes on the polished sod;
15 Sometimes he rode me on his back
Dipping and rising to his plod.

I wanted to grow up and plough,
To close one eye, stiffen my arm.
All I ever did was follow
20 In his broad shadow round the farm.

I was a nuisance, tripping, falling,
Yapping always. But today
It is my father who keeps stumbling
Behind me, and will not go away.

Reading for meaning

"Follower" is an exploration of the changing relationship between Heaney and his father.

1 Most of this poem describes the skill and strength of Heaney's father. How do each of
   the following lines express his father's qualities?

   • His shoulders globed like a full sail strung

   • The horses strained at his clicking tongue

   • with a single pluck/Of reins, the sweating team turned round

   • Dipping and rising to his plod.

2 What do the following lines tell you about the young Seamus Heaney?
   - I stumbled in his hob-nailed wake
   - I was a nuisance, tripping, falling/Yapping always.

3 What kind of animal does the young Heaney remind you of?

4 How has the relationship changed according to the last two and a half lines?

Literary techniques

Heaney uses a number of images, including "shoulders globed like a full sail", "hob-nailed wake" and "dipping and rising to his plod", which imply that is father is like a great ship navigating the fields of the farm.

1 Why do you think Heaney chose this particular set of images? Do you find it effective?

2 How does Heaney express his father's power over the horses by using contrast?

3 Comment on Heaney's use of run-on lines for emphasis in this poem.

4 Line 5 contains a sentence without a verb. What is the effect of isolating the words "An expert" in this way?

5 The poem has a regular rhyme scheme. Why do you think Heaney uses partial rhymes, such as "wake" and "back", rather than full rhymes throughout?

6 In the second stanza there are a number of technical terms to do with horse ploughs. Why do you think Heaney chose to use them rather than more easily understood words?

7 The final phrase of the poem could be read in two possible ways: either the father is still alive and is a continuing burden to his son; or the father is dead and his son cannot escape from the memory of his father "stumbling". Which of these two views of the poem do you think is most likely? Explain your choice.

Themes

As in several of his autobiographical poems, Heaney records a change which is not necessarily for the better. The power and strength of Heaney's father have been taken away by time, and the roles of parent and child have been reversed. Heaney seems more saddened by the loss of his powerful father than the trouble that a weak and helpless parent might cause him.

At a Potato Digging

I

A mechanical digger wrecks the drill,
Spins up a dark shower of roots and mould.
Labourers swarm behind, stoop to fill
Wicker creels. Fingers go dead in the cold.

5 Like crows attacking crow-black fields, they stretch
A higgledy line from hedge to headland;
Some pairs keep breaking ragged ranks to fetch
A full creel to the pit and straighten, stand

Tall for a moment but soon stumble back
10 To fish a new load from the crumbled surf.
Heads bow, trunks bend, hands fumble towards
   the black
Mother. Processional stooping through the turf

Recurs mindlessly as autumn. Centuries
Of fear and homage to the famine god
15 Toughen the muscles behind their humbled knees,
Make a seasonal altar of the sod.

II

Flint-white, purple. They lie scattered
like inflated pebbles. Native
to the black hutch of clay
20 where the halved seed shot and clotted
these knobbed and slit-eyed tubers seem
the petrified hearts of drills. Split
by the spade, they show white as cream.

Good smells exude from crumbled earth.
25 The rough bark of humus erupts
knots of potatoes (a clean birth)
whose solid feel, whose wet inside
promises taste of ground and root.
To be piled in pits; live skulls, blind-eyed.

III

30 Live skulls, blind-eyed, balanced on
wild higgledy skeletons
scoured the land in 'forty-five,
wolfed the blighted root and died.

The new potato, sound as stone,
35 putrefied when it had lain
three days in the long clay pit.
Millions rotted along with it.

Mouths tightened in, eyes died hard,
faces chilled to a plucked bird.
40 In a million wicker huts
beaks of famine snipped at guts.

A people hungering from birth,
grubbing, like plants, in the bitch earth,
were grafted with a great sorrow.
45 Hope rotted like a marrow.

Stinking potatoes fouled the land,
pits turned pus into filthy mounds:
and where potato diggers are
you still smell the running sore.

IV

50 Under a gay flotilla of gulls
The rhythm deadens, the workers stop.
Brown bread and tea in bright canfuls
Are served for lunch. Dead-beat, they flop

Down in the ditch and take their fill,
55 Thankfully breaking timeless fasts;
Then, stretched on the faithless ground, spill
Libations of cold tea, scatter crumbs.

Reading for meaning

1 With a partner read and discuss the poem and briefly state what each section is about.

2 What time of year does the first section describe?

3 What prompts the harvesters to work so hard?

4 What happens to the potatoes after they are picked?

5 What were living conditions like for people in Ireland in 1845?

6 How does the memory of the potato blight affect modern behaviour?

Literary techniques

1 What simile is used in the second stanza to describe the workers? How effective is it?

2 What metaphor concerning the field is implied by the mention of "creels" and the line "fish a new load from the crumbled surf"?

3 What do the terms "processional", "homage" and "altar" imply about the attitude of the workers to their task?

4 What does Heaney's choice of words to describe potatoes in the second section show about them and their importance?

5 How does Heaney use repetition to make the transition from the second to the third section shocking?

6 What is famine likened to in section 3?

7 Explain as fully as you can how Heaney uses disease imagery to convey the effects of the famine in section 3.

8 Discuss two possible interpretations of "breaking timeless fasts" in section 4.

9 The earth is described as "Mother" in section 1 and "bitch" in section 3. What does this change imply about the earth? How do the workers treat the earth in section 4?

10 Why do you think Heaney's scheme of rhymes and half-rhymes becomes noticeably tighter (using couplets) in section 3?

Themes

Heaney combines several of his characteristic themes in this poem: his links with the past; the idea of decay; and the nature of agricultural existence. In spite of the nominal Christianity of the people of Northern Ireland, Heaney suggests that their great sufferings in the past have given them an almost pagan relationship with the soil. They depend upon it and treat it with both fear and respect, just as ancient peoples did. As in his other agricultural poems Heaney emphasises the hard work done by farmers, but here he suggests the harshness of their underlying motivation: the fear of famine and death.

Gillian Clarke was born in 1937 in Cardiff and has lived in Wales for most of her life. She is a broadcaster, freelance writer and lecturer, and has published many highly successful collections of poetry. She edited the Anglo-Welsh Review from 1975 to 1984, and currently teaches on the MA course in Creative Writing at the University of Glamorgan.

Catrin

I can remember you, child,
As I stood in a hot, white
Room at the window watching
The people and cars taking
5 Turn at the traffic lights.
I can remember you, our first
Fierce confrontation, the tight
Red rope of love which we both
Fought over. It was a square
10 Environmental blank, disinfected
Of paintings or toys. I wrote
All over the walls with my
Words, coloured the clean squares
With the wild, tender circles
15 Of our struggle to become
Separate. We want, we shouted,
To be two, to be ourselves.

Neither won nor lost the struggle
In the glass tank clouded with feelings
20 Which changed us both. Still I am fighting
You off, as you stand there
With your straight, strong, long
Brown hair and your rosy,
Defiant glare, bringing up
25 From the heart's pool that old rope,
Tightening about my life,
Trailing love and conflict,
As you ask may you skate
In the dark, for one more hour.

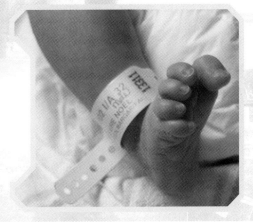

Reading for meaning

1 Where do you think the "hot, white room" was?

2 What was the speaker's "first fierce confrontation" with her daughter?

3 What is meant by the "tight red rope"?

4 How was the room decorated?

5 What did the mother and daughter want out of their struggle?

6 How old do you think the daughter is in the present of the poem?

7 How does the mother feel about letting her go out in the dark?

8 Has the relationship between mother and daughter changed a great deal over time?

Literary techniques

The poem is divided into two halves, one in the past and one in the present.

1 What impression is created by the descriptions of people passing in the street, the "hot, white room" and the "the glass tank clouded with feelings" in the first part of the poem?

2 How does this contrast with the environment in the second part of the poem where the daughter asks if she may "skate in the dark, for one more hour"?

3 What is the significance of the mother bringing sound and colour to the "environmental blank" of the labour ward in the process of giving birth to her child?

4 How is the umbilical cord described in the first part of the poem? How is its mental equivalent described in the second part of the poem? What do the changes in the image suggest?

5 Comment on the way Gillian Clarke builds up descriptions in this poem.

   • How effective is the description in lines 1–5 in setting the scene?

   • Why has the poet chosen this particular way of describing Catrin in the second stanza?

Themes

"That old rope ... trailing love and conflict" is at the heart of this poem. Mothers and children are joined at birth by the umbilical cord, but the cord must be cut if the child is to survive and grow. Similarly, mothers and their children are bound together later in life by love and dependency and it is just as necessary for the bond to be broken if the child is to prosper. The problem for the mother in this poem is knowing when to let go.

Baby-sitting

I am sitting in a strange room listening
For the wrong baby. I don't love
This baby. She is sleeping a snuffly
Roseate, bubbling sleep; she is fair;
5 She is a perfectly acceptable child.
I am afraid of her. If she wakes
She will hate me. She will shout
Her hot midnight rage, her nose
Will stream disgustingly and the perfume
10 Of her breath will fail to enchant me.
To her I will represent absolute
Abandonment. For her it will be worse
Than for the lover cold in lonely
Sheets; worse than for the woman who waits
15 A moment to collect her dignity
Beside the bleached bone in the terminal ward.
As she rises sobbing from the monstrous land
Stretching for milk-familiar comforting,
She will find me and between us two
20 It will not come. It will not come.

Reading for meaning

1 In what sense is the baby in the poem "the wrong baby"?

2 Why is the speaker afraid of the baby?

3 How will the baby react to the speaker, if it wakes? Why?

4 According to the poem, how serious is it for a baby to wake up and not find its mother?

5 What does the speaker feel she cannot provide?

Literary techniques

This poem is as much an exploration of the baby's feelings as it is of the baby-sitter's.

1 Make a list of the words used to describe the baby's feelings.

2 Make a similar list of the words used to describe the baby-sitter's feelings.

3 What do you notice about the intensity of the baby's feelings as compared to the baby-sitter's?

4 How do the baby's feelings compare with the vision of "snuffly roseate, bubbling sleep" given in stanza 1?

5 Why do you think Gillian Clarke uses two very adult images of abandonment in stanza 2?

6 How does the poet use alliteration and a run-on line in stanza 2 to emphasise "absolute abandonment"?

7 What other familiar images does the poem use?

8 Why do you think Gillian Clarke has repeated the phrase "It will not come" at the end of the poem?

Themes

"Baby-sitting" starts off by exploring the rather unexpected feelings of a baby-sitter with a small child, but it is apparent that the fears of the baby-sitter are caused by her knowledge of how the child will feel if it wakes up. In describing these feelings Gillian Clarke gives them the full weight of mature, adult emotions and shows that a commonplace act for a parent, leaving a child in someone else's care, can be a moment of major trauma for a child.

Mali

Three years ago to the hour, the day she was born,
that unmistakable brim and tug of the tide
I'd thought was over. I drove
the twenty miles of summer lanes,
5 my daughter cursing Sunday cars,
and the lazy swish of a dairy herd
rocking so slowly home.

Something in the event,
late summer heat overspilling into harvest,
10 apples reddening on heavy trees,
the lanes sweet with brambles
and our fingers purple,
then the child coming easy,
too soon, in the wrong place,
15 things seasonal and out of season
towed home a harvest moon.
My daughter's daughter
a day old under an umbrella on the beach
late-comer at summer's festival,
20 and I'm hooked again, life-sentenced.
Even the sea could not draw me from her.

This year I bake her a cake like our house,
and old trees blossom
with balloons and streamers.
25 We celebrate her with a cup
of cold blue ocean,
candles at twilight, and three drops of,
probably, last blood.

Reading for meaning

1 Who was born three years ago?

2 What problems occurred just before the birth?

3 How did the child's birth fit in with the natural rhythm of the year?

4 How did it not fit in with what was expected?

5 What had caused their fingers to be purple?

6 How has the birth of her granddaughter affected the speaker?

7 Briefly describe how the granddaughter's third birthday was celebrated.

Literary techniques

The poem makes several references to tides, which are caused by the gravitational attraction of the moon and, to a lesser extent, the sun.

1 What does the "tug" of the tide represent in the first stanza?

2 What had the speaker assumed about this "tug" before the birth of her granddaughter?

3 What does the speaker mean when she describes her daughter as a "harvest moon"?

4 What is the significance of the sea being powerless to "draw me from her"?

Other images in the poem emphasise life and vitality.

5 What late summer fruits are mentioned or referred to?

6 What is the significance of the fact that "old trees blossom" with the decorations for the party?

7 What does blood represent in the final image of the poem?

Themes

This poem resembles "Catrin" in its description of the bond between the speaker and a child. But in "Catrin" the bond was very close and a source of conflict. In this poem the bond is very strong, but it operates at a distance and seems characterised by joy. You could say that the difference between the two poems is the difference between a parent's and a grandparent's love for a child.

A Difficult Birth, Easter 1998

An old ewe that somehow till this year
had given the ram the slip. We thought her barren.
Good Friday, and the Irish peace deal close,
and tonight she's serious, restless and hoofing the straw.
5 We put off the quiet supper and bottle of wine
we'd planned, to celebrate if the news is good.

Her waters broke an hour ago and she's sipped
her own lost salty ocean from the ground.
While they slog it out in Belfast, eight decades
10 since Easter 1916, exhausted, tamed by pain,
she licks my fingers with a burning tongue,
lies down again. Two hooves and a muzzle.

But the lamb won't come. You phone for help
and step into the lane to watch for car lights.
15 This is when the whitecoats come to the women,
well-meaning, knowing best, with their needles and forceps.
So I ease my fingers in, take the slippery head
in my right hand, two hooves in my left.

We strain together, harder than we dared.
20 I feel a creak in the limbs and pull till he comes
in a syrupy flood. She drinks him, famished, and you find us
peaceful, at a cradling that might have been a death.
Then the second lamb slips through her opened door,
the stone rolled away.

Reading for meaning

1 Why had the old ewe not produced any lambs? What had the speaker assumed about
   her?

2 What were the speaker and her husband planning to do if the news about the peace deal
   was good?

3 What is the problem with the delivery of the lamb?

4 Who are the "whitecoats"? What does the speaker dislike about them?

5 What seems to have been the problem with the birth of the lamb?

Literary techniques

One of the most unusual things about this poem is the way it uses an everyday event in the lives of farmers to comment on larger political events.

1 How might the phrase "a difficult birth" be applied to the Good Friday peace agreement of 1998?

2 What two other Easters are mentioned in the poem? What effect do all these references to Easter have?

3 The phrase "exhausted, tamed by pain" describes the ewe, but what comment does it make on the history of Ireland since 1916?

4 The birth of the first lamb is "difficult" but the second lamb "slips through". What does this suggest about the possible future of Ireland if the Good Friday agreement succeeds?

A second striking element in the poem is its comment on the process of childbirth.

5 How are the ram and the husband similar when it comes to the birth of the lambs?

6 Why do you think Gillian Clarke uses the metonym "whitecoats" to refer to doctors? What does it suggest about them?

7 Why does she pick on "needles" and "forceps" as the principal instruments used by doctors?

8 What does the fact that only females are involved in the successful birth suggest about the political message of the poem?

9 The imagery of the poem is worth noting. What is implied by the following?
   • The sheep sipping her "lost salty ocean"
   • The sheep's "burning tongue"
   • The lamb coming in a "syrupy flood"
   • Saying that the sheep "drinks" the lamb.

10 What comment could you make about the flow of liquid in the poem?

11 What other religious scene is evoked by the husband, a shepherd, finding his wife in a stable, at "a cradling that might have been a death"? What comment about all births does this phrase imply?

Key Terms

Metonym – a word describing one aspect of a thing which is used to refer to the whole thing, for example "the crown" is used to refer to a monarch.

Themes

The birth of a lamb is the immediate occasion for the poem, but Gillian Clarke uses this to reflect on past and present political developments in Ireland. She also touches on issues of male and female attitudes to birth in the third stanza, and a religious dimension is provided in the fourth.

The Field-Mouse

Summer, and the long grass is a snare drum.
The air hums with jets.
Down at the end of the meadow,
far from the radio's terrible news,
5 we cut the hay. All afternoon
its wave breaks before the tractor blade.
Over the hedge our neighbour travels his field
in a cloud of lime, drifting our land
with a chance gift of sweetness.

10 The child comes running through the killed flowers,
his hands a nest of quivering mouse,
its black eyes two sparks burning.
We know it will die and ought to finish it off.
It curls in agony big as itself
15 and the star goes out in its eye.
Summer in Europe, the field's hurt,
and the children kneel in long grass,
staring at what we have crushed.

Before day's done the field lies bleeding,
20 the dusk garden inhabited by the saved, voles,
frogs, a nest of mice. The wrong that woke
from a rumour of pain won't heal,
and we can't face the newspapers.
All night I dream the children dance in grass
25 their bones brittle as mouse-ribs, the air
stammering with gunfire, my neighbour turned
stranger, wounding my land with stones.

Reading for meaning

1 What is happening in the speaker's part of the world?

2 What seems to be happening elsewhere in Europe?

3 What is the speaker's neighbour doing?

4 What do you think the child expects the speaker to do for the injured mouse?

5 What should she do with it?

6 What other animals are affected by the hay cutting?

7 How does the speaker's dream connect what has happened on the farm with what is happening in the world?

8 What has happened to the neighbour in the speaker's dream?

Literary techniques

Like "A Difficult Birth" this poem connects everyday events with those happening in the wider world.

1 In stanzas 1 and 2, how does the speaker see events on the farm as a metaphor for events in Europe?

2 In stanza 3, is using a dream/nightmare an effective way of making a connection between these events?

3 The reaction of the children to the suffering of small animals is a metaphor for how we respond to people affected by war. How effective do you find this technique?

4 The suffering brought about by war is emphasised by the personification of the field. Find three examples of this and explain which one of them you find most effective.

5 What simile makes an explicit connection between the injured mouse and the speaker's children?

Themes

"The Field-Mouse" examines the fear that often accompanies a parent's love for a child. Adults naturally wish to protect their children from harm and distress, but there are some things, such as injury and death, that parents have little or no power over. In a peaceful country such fears are usually confined to accidents, but civil wars, like the one that broke out in the former Yugoslavia, mean that even a neighbour can become a threat.

October

Wind in the poplars and a broken branch,
a dead arm in the bright trees. Five poplars
tremble gradually to gold. The stone face
of the lion darkens in a sharp shower,
5 his dreadlocks of lobelia grown long,
tangled, more brown now than blue-eyed.

My friend dead and the graveyard at Orcop –
her short ride to the hawthorn hedge, lighter
than hare-bones on men's shoulders, our faces
10 stony, rain, weeping in the air. The grave
deep as a well takes the earth's thud, the slow
fall of flowers.

Over the page the pen
runs faster than wind's white steps over grass.
For a while health feels like pain. Then panic
15 running the fields, the grass, the racing leaves
ahead of light, holding that robin's eye
in the laurel, hydrangeas' faded green.
I must write like the wind, year after year
passing my death-day, winning ground.

Reading for meaning

1 What aspects of the poplar trees tell you that it is autumn?

2 What is happening to the lobelias at this time of year?

3 In what way is the funeral "autumnal"?

4 In what way might "health" feel "like pain"?

5 Why does the speaker feel compelled to write poetry?

Literary techniques

1 Gillian Clarke connects three events, the month of October, a funeral and the need to write poems. What do these three things have in common?

2 In what ways does the description of the trees prefigure the scene at the funeral?

3 How is the description of the stone lion similar to the description of the people at the funeral?

4 How does the third stanza differ from the first two in its tone and what it describes?

5 The poet's use of imagery is quite striking. Comment on the following images:

- a broken branch, a dead arm in the bright trees
- poplars tremble gradually to gold
- lighter than hare-bones on men's shoulders
- the grave deep as a well
- faster than wind's white steps over grass
- year after year passing my death-day.

6 What kind of things does Gillian Clarke say she must capture in her writing? Are these kinds of things mentioned in the earlier part of the poem?

Themes

This simple, reflective poem is a response to the death in both the natural and the human world. In the natural world, death in winter is always followed by new life in spring, but for non-religious human beings each day we live only brings us closer to our personal end. Gillian Clarke's response to this rather bleak prospect is to try and create something permanent in her poetry.

On the Train

Cradled through England between flooded fields
rocking, rocking the rails, my head-phones on,
the black box of my Walkman on the table.
Hot tea trembles in its plastic cup.
5 I'm thinking of you waking in our bed
thinking of me on the train. Too soon to phone.

The radio speaks in the suburbs, in commuter towns,
in cars unloading children at school gates,
is silenced in dark parkways down the line
10 before locks click and footprints track the frost
and trains slide out of stations in the dawn
dreaming their way towards the blazing bone-ship.

The Vodaphone you are calling
may have been switched off.
15 Please call later. And calling later,
calling later their phones ring in the rubble
and in the rubble of suburban kitchens
the wolves howl into silent telephones.

I phone. No answer. Where are you now?
20 The train moves homeward through the morning.
Tonight I'll be home safe, but talk to me, please.
Pick up the phone. Today I'm tolerant
of mobiles. Let them say it. I'll say it too.
Darling, I'm on the train.

Reading for meaning

1 Where is the speaker at the start of the poem?

2 What time of day do you think it is? Provide evidence from the poem for your answer.

3 What are the trains said to be dreaming their way towards? How might a train dream?

4 How does the tone of the poem change after this line?

5 What does the speaker worry about when there is no answer to her call?

6 What is the normal reaction of the speaker to people who say "I'm on the train"?

7 Why does she not feel like this today?

Literary techniques

1 What effect does Gillian Clarke achieve through the use of rhythm, repetition and alliteration in the first stanza?

2 Consider the possible meanings of "blazing bone-ship". If the bone-ship is a train, in what senses might it be blazing? What does calling a train a "bone-ship" emphasise about its passengers? Do you consider this image to be positive, negative or ambiguous?

3 Explain as fully as you can the differences between the language used by the Vodaphone answering service and the language used in the other parts of the poem.

4 How major a disaster is implied by the image of wolves in suburban English kitchens?

5 Why are there three separate sentences in the first line of the fourth stanza?

6 What technique does Gillian Clarke use in the final line of the poem? Why is it effective here?

Themes

"On the Train" is a not very serious poem about the anxiety felt by someone separated from his or her loved one. It is consciously contemporary with its mention of brand names such as "Vodaphone" and "Walkman" and it makes use of a well-known and generally condemned cliché in its final line. In expressing anxiety the poem goes over the top, imagining not just a single personal disaster but the breakdown of civilisation as we currently know it. Perhaps there is an attempt here to prick our smugness about technological advances and remind us that we are never really very far away from disaster.

Cold Knap Lake

We once watched a crowd
pull a drowned child from the lake.
Blue-lipped and dressed in water's long green silk
she lay for dead.

5 Then kneeling on the earth,
a heroine, her red head bowed,
her wartime cotton frock soaked,
my mother gave a stranger's child her breath.
The crowd stood silent,
10 drawn by the dread of it.

The child breathed, bleating
and rosy in my mother's hands.
My father took her home to a poor house
and watched her thrashed for almost drowning.

15 Was I there?
Or is that troubled surface something else
shadowy under the dipped fingers of willows
where satiny mud blooms in cloudiness
after the treading, heavy webs of swans
20 as their wings beat and whistle on the air?

All lost things lie under closing water
in that lake with the poor man's daughter.

Reading for meaning

1 What do you think the poet means when she says "a crowd" pulled the child from the lake?

2 Who gave the child the kiss of life?

3 How did the crowd react?

4 Why do you think the girl was beaten for almost drowning? Is parental anger a common reaction when a child gets into trouble?

5 Why do you think the speaker is uncertain about whether she was present at the beating?

Literary techniques

1 Find two examples in the first eight lines where Gillian Clarke holds back information to create suspense.

2 Discuss whether you think "gave ... her breath" is a better expression than "gave the kiss of life".

3 How does Gillian Clarke create tension at the end of the second stanza?

4 Why do you think the line "Was I there?" is shorter than all the others in the poem?

5 What comparison does Gillian Clarke make between memory and the surface of the lake?

6 Why do you think the poem ends with a rhyming couplet?

Themes

The theme of this poem is memory. The poem begins with a vivid memory from the speaker's childhood and then records an equally dramatic sequel. However, the speaker is unable to tell whether the memory of the beating is a real one or simply something based on stories told in the family. Gillian Clarke uses the surface of the lake as a metaphor for the uncertainty of memory. Some details are clear but others are clouded by the passage of time.

Carol Ann Duffy was born in Glasgow in 1955. She
had her first work published when she was sixteen,
and since graduating in Philosophy from Liverpool
University in 1977, she has published several highly
successful collections of poetry and won many
awards, including an OBE. She has also written
plays and an anthology for teenagers.

Havisham

Beloved sweetheart bastard. Not a day since then
I haven't wished him dead. Prayed for it
so hard I've dark green pebbles for eyes,
ropes on the back of my hands I could strangle with.

5 Spinster. I stink and remember. Whole days
in bed cawing Nooooo at the wall; the dress
yellowing, trembling if I open the wardrobe;
the slewed mirror, full-length, her, myself, who did this

to me? Puce curses that are sounds not words.
10 Some nights better, the lost body over me,
my fluent tongue in its mouth in its ear
then down till I suddenly bite awake. Love's

hate behind a white veil; a red balloon bursting
in my face. Bang. I stabbed at a wedding-cake.
15 Give me a male corpse for a long slow honeymoon.
Don't think it's only the heart that b-b-b-breaks.

BACKGROUND

Miss Havisham is a character from the novel *Great Expectations* by Charles Dickens. She is an
eccentric recluse after having been jilted on her wedding day. She orders all the clocks in her
home to be stopped at the moment she heard the news of her desertion and she has
preserved everything as it was at that moment, even to the extent of spending the rest of
her life with one shoe on and one shoe off. In order to take revenge on men Miss Havisham
adopts the beautiful Estella whose mission in life is to break men's hearts.

Reading for meaning

1 Why do you think the title of this poem is "Havisham" rather than "Miss Havisham" as she is known in the novel? (Think about what used to happen to a woman's name when she married.)

2 How has being jilted affected Miss Havisham physically?

3 How would you say it has affected her mentally?

4 What is the significance of Miss Havisham looking in the mirror and seeing "her, myself"?

5 Does she still find the man who jilted her attractive? How can you tell?

6 What does she mostly want to happen to him?

7 What do you think the "red balloon" represents?

8 How has being jilted affected Miss Havisham's attitude to all men?

Literary techniques

1 What kind of phrase is "Beloved sweetheart bastard"? Are there any further examples of this construction in the poem? What do they show about Miss Havisham's feelings?

2 Why is "spinster" in a sentence on its own? What does the lack of a verb indicate?

3 Miss Havisham describes herself as "cawing" and uttering curses that are "sounds not words". What does this show about the damage that has been done to her as a human being?

4 Why are the words "Nooooo" and "b-b-b-breaks" written in this manner? How do these words help us to imagine her situation? How do you respond to them as a reader?

5 What do you understand by Miss Havisham's question "who did this to me?" when she is looking in the mirror? Is her present state her own fault or that of the man who jilted her?

6 The word "Bang" seems to refer to both the "red balloon bursting" and to her stabbing the wedding cake. Why do you think these two images are linked?

Themes

"Havisham" describes a fierce hatred born out of love, so that, to some extent, the continued existence of the hatred reveals the presence of the original love. Unfortunately, in the absence of the man who hurt her Miss Havisham directs the punishment for her betrayal at herself. Readers of *Great Expectations* will know that Carol Ann Duffy's view of Miss Havisham differs from the portrait provided by Charles Dickens. In the novel there is no suggestion that she still loves the man who jilted her and she spends most of her time plotting to hurt men in general through the agency of her beautiful ward, Estella. The poem is therefore inspired by the novel but is meant to exist outside it.

Elvis's Twin Sister

Are you lonesome tonight? Do you miss me tonight?

Elvis is alive and she's female: Madonna

In the convent, y'all,
I tend the gardens,
watch things grow,
pray for the immortal soul
5 of rock 'n' roll.

They call me
Sister Presley here.
The Reverend Mother
digs the way I move my hips
10 just like my brother.

Gregorian chant
drifts out across the herbs
Pascha nostrum immolatus est ...
I wear a simple habit,
15 darkish hues,

a wimple with a novice-sewn
lace band, a rosary,
a chain of keys,
a pair of good and sturdy
20 blue suede shoes.

I think of it
as Graceland here,
a land of grace.
It puts my trademark slow lopsided smile
25 back on my face.

Lawdy.
I'm alive and well.
Long time since I walked
down Lonely Street
30 towards Heartbreak Hotel.

Carol Ann Duffy

118

BACKGROUND

Elvis Aaron Presley (1935–77) was perhaps the most famous rock and roll singer of all time. He is credited with introducing rock and roll to white audiences and at one stage his dancing was considered so shocking that he was only shown above the waist on television. Famed as both a singer and film actor, he made his home at Graceland in Memphis, Tennessee. His recordings include *Heartbreak Hotel*, *Blue Suede Shoes* and *Jailhouse Rock*.

Pascha nostrum immolatus est – a Latin phrase from the Gregorian chant (unaccompanied singing that forms part of the church service). It means, "Our Easter Lamb is sacrificed."

Reading for meaning

1 What are Elvis's twin sister's main occupations?

2 What does the word "dig" mean in stanza 2?

3 How does Elvis's twin sister's dress contrast with that of her brother?

4 Why is it appropriate that Elvis's twin sister should be wearing blue suede shoes?

5 How is the convent similar to her brother's residence?

6 What does Elvis's twin sister have that her brother didn't seem to have, according to the last stanza?

Literary techniques

1 The poem contains at least three kinds of language: religious, southern American slang and everyday speech. Identify examples of each type of language and say why you think its use is effective.

2 The poem also alludes to several songs. What do these reveal about the life of Elvis's twin sister and that of her brother?

3 How does Carol Ann Duffy make use of the persona of Elvis's twin sister to comment on Elvis?

4 How well do you think the poem uses allusion to Elvis's lyrics to emphasise the contrast between Elvis and his twin sister?

5 Why do you think Carol Ann Duffy placed the two quotations at the beginning of the poem?

6 The poem's simple short lines enable the poet to make good use of run-ons for effect.

   • Find examples where the conclusion to a line is not what might have been expected.

   • How does this technique affect the tone of the poem?

Theme

This poem makes a simple contrast between fame and obscurity. It is clear that Elvis's twin sister has many of her brother's talents, but she has chosen to retire to a convent while her brother sought fame and fortune. Both siblings have been successful in gaining what they wanted from life, but Elvis's twin sister seems to have achieved greater happiness and peace.

Anne Hathaway

'Item I gyve unto my wife my second best bed...'
(from Shakespeare's will)

The bed we loved in was a spinning world
of forests, castles, torchlight, clifftops, seas
where he would dive for pearls. My lover's words
were shooting stars which fell to earth as kisses
5 on these lips; my body now a softer rhyme
to his, now echo, assonance; his touch
a verb dancing in the centre of a noun.
Some nights, I dreamed he'd written me, the bed
a page beneath his writer's hands. Romance
10 and drama played by touch, by scent, by taste.
In the other bed, the best, our guests dozed on,
dribbling their prose. My living laughing love –
I hold him in the casket of my widow's head
as he held me upon that next best bed.

Anne Hathaway (1557–1623) was the wife of William Shakespeare (1564–1616). For most of his working life Shakespeare lived in London, while Anne Hathaway remained in Stratford-upon-Avon. The couple had three children together, Susannah, Judith and Hamnet, and Shakespeare retired to Stratford-upon-Avon in the final years of his life. In the Elizabethan period the best bed would have been reserved for guests and so the second best bed would have been the one that a married couple shared. Shakespeare wrote 37 plays and numerous poems, including a collection of 153 sonnets. Shakespearean sonnets are characterised by the use of a rhyming couplet at the end.

Reading for meaning

1 What do you learn from this poem about the kind of writer that Shakespeare was?

2 What does this poem tell you about the quality of the relationship between Anne Hathaway and Shakespeare?

Literary techniques

1 The poem is written as a Shakespearean sonnet. Why is this appropriate?

2 The poem consists of a series of comparisons. Identify what each of the following is compared to:

   • the bed itself

   • Shakespeare's words

   • Anne Hathaway's body

   • Shakespeare's touch

   • the bed with Anne Hathaway in it

   • the romance and drama of Shakespeare and Anne Hathaway's love.

3 At the end of the poem Anne Hathaway states that she holds Shakespeare in the casket of her head. Is this an effective image? What kinds of objects are normally placed in caskets?

4 What use does Carol Ann Duffy make of the final rhyming couplet?

Themes

This is a lighthearted love poem which undermines the commonly held view that Anne Hathaway's marriage to Shakespeare was a rather distant and cool one. The poem's playful use of imagery, affectionate tone and sincere emotion reflect Anne Hathaway's love and loss.

Salome

I'd done it before
(and doubtless I'll do it again,
sooner or later)
woke up with a head on the pillow beside me – whose? –
5 what did it matter?
Good-looking, of course, dark hair, rather matted;
the reddish beard several shades lighter;
with very deep lines around the eyes,
from pain, I'd guess, maybe laughter;
10 and a beautiful crimson mouth that obviously knew
how to flatter ...
which I kissed ...
Colder than pewter.
Strange. What was his name? Peter?

15 Simon? Andrew? John? I knew I'd feel better
for tea, dry toast, no butter,
so rang for the maid.
And, indeed, her innocent clatter
of cups and plates,
20 her clearing of clutter,
her regional patter,
were just what I needed –
hungover and wrecked as I was from a night on the batter.

Never again!
25 I needed to clean up my act,
get fitter,
cut out the booze and the fags and the sex.
Yes. And as for the latter,
it was time to turf out the blighter,
30 the beater or biter,
who'd come like a lamb to the slaughter
to Salome's bed.

In the mirror, I saw my eyes glitter.
I flung back the sticky red sheets,
35 and there, like I said – and ain't life a bitch –
was his head on a platter.

BACKGROUND

In the New Testament Salome was the daughter of Herodias, the mistress of King Herod. John the Baptist offended Herodias by preaching against her immoral behaviour, and so when King Herod asked to see Salome dance, her mother told her to ask for the head of John the Baptist as payment. The agreement was made and after Salome's dance the head of John the Baptist was brought in on a plate. No other versions of the story suggest that Salome took the head to her bed with her.

Reading for meaning

1 What does Salome assume about the head beside her at the beginning of the poem?

2 Was she used to this sort of thing?

3 Why couldn't she remember the man's name?

4 What was the real reason for the coldness of the man's lips? What do you think Salome assumed?

5 Were tea and "fags" available in Israel in the first century AD?

6 What is the usual meaning of "like a lamb to the slaughter"? Why is it rather an unfortunate turn of phrase in this case?

7 Who is life a "bitch" for? Salome or John the Baptist?

Literary techniques

One of the most striking aspects of this poem is its use of anachronism.

1 How is the language of the poem anachronistic? Give some examples.

2 What physical anachronisms does the poem contain?

3 What do you think is anachronistic about Salome's behaviour?

4 What do all of these examples suggest about how human behaviour changes over time?

5 What would you say was the tone of this poem? How is this helped by its use of colloquial language and a rather insistent rhyme scheme?

6 Given that John the Baptist is probably as famous for the way he died as for the way he lived, why do you think that there are so many rhymes with the word "platter" in the poem?

7 Who were Peter, Simon and Andrew in the New Testament? What does Salome's confusion about these names suggest about her knowledge of local developments in religion?

Themes

Salome has been the subject of stories, pictures, poems and plays for centuries but most of these have focussed on her dance and not on the morning after. Salome committed a great crime in causing the death of John the Baptist, but she did not care personally about her actions. She danced to please her mother and used her sexuality to gain Herod's compliance in her mother's revenge. The Salome of the poem seems to be a modern embodiment of such thoughtless sexuality. In her early morning forgetfulness she merely thinks that she has succeeded in attracting a man to her bed, but by the end of the poem the full consequences of her actions the night before are revealed.

Before You Were Mine

I'm ten years away from the corner you laugh on
with your pals, Maggie McGeeney and Jean Duff.
The three of you bend from the waist, holding
each other, or your knees, and shriek at the pavement.
5 Your polka-dot dress blows round your legs. Marilyn.

I'm not here yet. The thought of me doesn't occur
in the ballroom with the thousand eyes, the fizzy, movie tomorrows
the right walk home could bring. I knew you would dance
like that. Before you were mine, your Ma stands at the close
10 with a hiding for the late one. You reckon it's worth it.

The decade ahead of my loud, possessive yell was the best one, eh?
I remember my hands in those high-heeled red shoes, relics,
and now your ghost clatters toward me over George Square
till I see you, clear as scent, under the tree,
15 with its lights, and whose small bites on your neck, sweetheart?

Cha cha cha! You'd teach me the steps on the way home from Mass,
stamping stars from the wrong pavement. Even then
I wanted the bold girl winking in Portobello, somewhere
in Scotland, before I was born. That glamorous love lasts
20 where you sparkle and waltz and laugh before you were mine.

Reading for meaning

1 In which decade was the speaker's mother a teenager?

2 What decade was the speaker in this poem born in?

3 How do you think the speaker found out about what her mother did with her friends ten years before the speaker was born?

4 Using evidence from the whole poem, describe what the speaker's mother was like as a teenager.

5 What was life like for her after her daughter was born?

6 In the poem who seems to regret the loss of the mother's glamorous life: the mother or the daughter?

Literary techniques

1 The poem deals with two sets of memories. Identify:
   • the memories that belong to the speaker
   • the ones that belongs to the speaker's mother.

2 What are the main differences between the two sets of memories?

3 How does the rhythm change in the "glamorous" sections?

4 What technique does Carol Ann Duffy use when she describes her mother's dancing shoes as "high-heeled red shoes, relics"?

5 Explain as fully as you can the image "I see you, clear as scent" in the third stanza. What does the image suggest about the way memory often works?

6 The poem has a generally steady rhythm, apart from at the end of each stanza. Why do you think this is, and why does stanza 4 not follow this pattern?

7 What use does Carol Ann Duffy make of "l" sounds (e.g. "glamorous love") in the last two lines of the poem?

Themes

This poem reflects an experience that many teenagers must share: the difference between parents as we know them and how they must have been when they were teenagers themselves. In Carol Ann Duffy's poem the difference between her mother's glamorous teenage years and her years as a parent is heightened by the mother's strict Catholicism and the fact that the end of the 1950s and beginning of the 1960s were years of comparative austerity. The child in this poem seems quite possessive: she wants both her mother as she is and as she was.

We Remember Your Childhood Well

Nobody hurt you. Nobody turned off the light and argued
with somebody else all night. The bad man on the moors
was only a movie you saw. Nobody locked the door.

Your questions were answered fully. No. That didn't occur.
5 You couldn't sing anyway, cared less. The moment's a blur, a *Film Fun*
laughing itself to death in the coal fire. Anyone's guess.

Nobody forced you. You wanted to go that day. Begged. You chose
the dress. Here are the pictures, look at you. Look at us all,
smiling and waving, younger. The whole thing is inside your head.

10 What you recall are impressions; we have the facts. We called the tune.
The secret police of your childhood were older and wiser than you, bigger
than you. Call back the sound of their voices. Boom. Boom. Boom.

Nobody sent you away. That was an extra holiday, with people
you seemed to like. They were firm, there was nothing to fear.
15 There was none but yourself to blame if it ended in tears.

What does it matter now? No, no, nobody left the skidmarks of sin
on your soul and laid you wide open for Hell. You were loved.
Always. We did what was best. We remember your childhood well.

Reading for meaning

This poem consists of one half of a conversation between a child and her parents. The
child seems to be making a number of accusations about her past and the parents are
responding to them.

1 What accusations does the child seem to have made in stanza 1?

2 What two grievances are mentioned in stanza 2?

3 What event is being discussed in stanza 3? What did the parents do to offend
their child?

4 How do the memories change between stanzas 1 and 3?

5 How does the conversation change in stanza 4?

6 What went wrong in stanza 5? What does this stanza reveal about adult attitudes to
children when this poem was written?

7 What have the parents been accused of in stanza 6? How is this different from the other
complaints made by the child in the poem?

Literary techniques

1 Do you think it is appropriate that the child's voice is not heard in the poem? Give reasons for your answer.

2 How is the child's language reflected in the poem?

3 Discuss some of ways the parents attempt to argue with their child. What is their commonest strategy?

4 In the lines "a *Film Fun* laughing itself to death in the coal fire", whose perspective is being presented? Why might some people find the idea behind this image disturbing?

5 In stanza 4, what is the significance of the fact that the parents claim to know how the child saw the world?

6 How is this impression reinforced by the choice of language in this stanza? What is the effect of the repeated "Boom. Boom. Boom"?

7 Under what circumstances do tyres leave skidmarks? What does this image imply about the damage done to the child?

8 What is the effect of the numerous short sentences at the end of the poem?

Themes

This poem makes an interesting contrast with "Before You Were Mine". In that poem the child is the custodian of the family memories and appears to hold them dear in spite of being a little envious of her mother's former glamour. "In We Remember Your Childhood Well" the child's attempt to share her memories is met with incomprehension and denial. The reader might sympathise with their denial of some of the child's early memories, as they seem to be based on only partial information, but they express no understanding of their child's point of view when her memories become clearer. They insist that their point of view is the correct one and that the child's subjective experience does not count. By stanza 4 they have become bullies who rely on their strength and power and describe themselves as "secret police".

Behind the poem lies the simple observation that people remember things differently. What makes this poem disturbing is the refusal of the parents to acknowledge the validity of their daughter's experience.

Education for Leisure

Today I am going to kill something. Anything.
I have had enough of being ignored and today
I am going to play God. It is an ordinary day,
a sort of grey with boredom stirring in the streets.

5 I squash a fly against the window with my thumb.
We did that at school. Shakespeare. It was in
another language and now the fly is in another language.
I breathe out talent on the glass to write my name.

I am a genius. I could be anything at all, with half
10 the chance. But today I am going to change the world.
Something's world. The cat avoids me. The cat
knows I am a genius, and has hidden itself.

I pour the goldfish down the bog. I pull the chain.
I see that it is good. The budgie is panicking.
15 Once a fortnight, I walk the two miles into town
for signing on. They don't appreciate my autograph.

There is nothing left to kill. I dial the radio
and tell the man he's talking to a superstar.
He cuts me off. I get our bread-knife and go out.
20 The pavements glitter suddenly. I touch your arm.

Reading for meaning

1 Explain what you understand by the phrase "play God".

2 Why does the speaker want to kill things?

3 What do you think the speaker means when he says the fly is "in another language"?

4 How does killing the fly make the speaker feel?

5 Why do you think the speaker values being feared by the cat and the budgie?

6 How does the speaker see himself in relation to the "ordinary" world?

7 Why do you think "the pavements glitter suddenly"?

8 Explain as fully as you can why you think the poem is called "Education for Leisure".

Carol Ann Duffy

Literary techniques

1 This poem is written in the present tense, as if recording the speaker's thoughts and actions as they occur.

   • What is the advantage of this technique?

   • Where in the poem is it most effective?

2 The poem also has a number of references to the past. Identify these references and explain what they add to our knowledge of the speaker.

3 The poem contains a number of verbless sentences. Identify these sentences and explain the effect of having sentences with no "action" words in them.

4 What is the effect of following "Today I am going to change the world" with "Something's world" on the next line?

5 Can you find other examples of very grand claims placed next to very ordinary circumstances or achievements?

6 The speaker has had some education as he is able to refer to both Shakespeare and the Bible. How do these allusions help to emphasise the bleakness of the speaker's circumstance?

7 Do you think the speaker's education was likely to help him to cope with a life of unemployment?

Themes

Like "Stealing", this poem is an attempt to see the world from the point of view of someone who does not fit into "normal" patterns of behaviour. Carol Ann Duffy does not attempt to enlist our sympathy for the killer in this poem but she does provide some clues for his behaviour. She suggests that the education that the speaker has received has not equipped him for the life he has to lead of unemployed "leisure".

Stealing

The most unusual thing I ever stole? A snowman.
Midnight. He looked magnificent; a tall, white mute
beneath the winter moon. I wanted him, a mate
with a mind as cold as the slice of ice
5 within my own brain. I started with the head.

Better off dead than giving in, not taking
what you want. He weighed a ton; his torso,
frozen stiff, hugged to my chest, a fierce chill
piercing my gut. Part of the thrill was knowing
10 that children would cry in the morning. Life's tough.

Sometimes I steal things I don't need. I joy-ride cars
to nowhere, break into houses just to have a look.
I'm a mucky ghost, leave a mess, maybe pinch a camera.
I watch my gloved hand twisting the doorknob.
15 A stranger's bedroom. Mirrors. I sigh like this – *Aah*.

It took some time. Reassembled in the yard,
he didn't look the same. I took a run
and booted him. Again. Again. My breath ripped out
in rags. It seems daft now. Then I was standing
20 alone amongst lumps of snow, sick of the world.

Boredom. Mostly I'm so bored I could eat myself.
One time, I stole a guitar and thought I might
learn to play. I nicked a bust of Shakespeare once,
flogged it, but the snowman was strangest.
25 You don't understand a word I'm saying, do you?

Reading for meaning

1 The poem begins with what appears to be an answer to a question. Who do you think is being addressed?

2 Why did the speaker want to steal the snowman?

3 What other reason did he have for taking it?

4 What did he do with the snowman in the end, after all his effort?

5 What else has the speaker stolen?

6 Why does he say he steals things?

7 Why do you think he steals things he doesn't want or need?

Literary techniques

1 The poem is written in regular five-line stanzas. How does Carol Ann Duffy vary the pace by using run-ons and occasional very brief sentences?

2 How else does she try to create the impression of ordinary speech in the poem?

3 What do "the winter moon", "ice", a "ghost", "mirrors" and "a bust of Shakespeare" all have in common?

4 What do these images suggest about the thief?

Themes

This poem is a dramatic monologue which deals with another outsider like the one in "Education for Leisure". The speaker in this poem does have a set of skills, but they place him outside normal society and in any case he doesn't seem able to connect with other people. He has chosen a lonely form of crime but he cannot resist leaving clues about his presence. He breathes on mirrors, makes a mess and enters rooms, but all his attempts at contact are bound to come to nothing. His attempt to take the snowman as a "mate" with something in common reveals the level of the speaker's desperation. The whole poem seems to be a conversation with someone, but as with so many of his possible contacts, the speaker deliberately sabotages communication at the end. "You don't understand a word I'm saying, do you?"

Author profile

Born in 1963, Simon Armitage is a prize-winning poet from West Yorkshire. In his poems, which are both imaginative and serious, he uses northern colloquialisms alongside standard English, often for ironic effect. He has published several highly successful books of poetry and prose, and also writes for television and radio.

from Book of Matches

Mother, any distance greater than a single span
requires a second pair of hands.
You come to help me measure windows, pelmets, doors,
the acres of the walls, the prairies of the floors.

5 You at the zero-end, me with the spool of tape, recording
length, reporting metres, centimetres back to base, then leaving
up the stairs, the line still feeding out, unreeling
years between us. Anchor. Kite.

I space-walk through the empty bedrooms, climb
10 the ladder to the loft, to breaking point, where something
has to give;
two floors below your fingertips still pinch
the last one-hundredth of an inch ... I reach
towards a hatch that opens on an endless sky
15 to fall or fly.

Reading for meaning

1 Why has the speaker's mother come to visit him?

2 What task is the mother given?

3 What tasks does the speaker perform?

4 How high does the speaker climb at the end of the poem?

5 What does the last line reveal about the speaker's feelings towards his mother?

Literary techniques

1 How does Armitage's use of lists help to convey the extent of his task?

2 What words in line 4 also convey the idea of a seemingly endless task?

3 Armitage uses two single-word sentences in line 8 to describe the relationship between himself and his mother. What is implied by the metaphors he has chosen?

4 Why do you think he has separated the two images in this way?

5 Comment on Armitage's use of the term "space-walk" in line 9. What images does it suggest?

6 Why do you think the tape measure is described as being at "breaking point"?

7 How does Armitage's choice of the word "pinch" in line 12 affect the way we understand the relationship between mother and son? What is the effect of the strong rhyme with "inch" on the next line?

8 Most of the poem has a regular rhythm, but exceptions to this can be found on lines 8 and 11. Explain why you think Armitage chose to break up the rhythm in these two lines.

Themes

The connection between a mother and her child is a strong one that is not easily broken. For the mother there is the danger of clinging on for too long. For the child there is both frustration at being held on to and fear of what freedom might bring.

from Book of Matches

My father thought it bloody queer,
the day I rolled home with a ring of silver in my ear
half hidden by a mop of hair. "You've lost your head.
If that's how easily you're led
5 you should've had it through your nose instead."

And even then I hadn't had the nerve to numb
the lobe with ice, then drive a needle through the skin,
then wear a safety-pin. It took a jeweller's gun
to pierce the flesh, and then a friend
10 to thread a sleeper in, and where it slept
the hole became a sore, became a wound, and wept.

At twenty-nine, it comes as no surprise to hear
my own voice breaking like a tear, released like water,
cried from way back in the spiral of the ear. *If I were you,*
15 *I'd take it out and leave it out next year.*

Reading for meaning

1 Why is the speaker's father upset by his son wearing an earring?

2 Why does the father say that the speaker should have had a ring in his nose instead of his ear?

3 At the time, what was the "proper" way to pierce your ears?

4 What did the speaker do and what went wrong?

5 How does the speaker feel when he eventually gives up wearing the earring at the age of twenty-nine?

Literary techniques

1 The poem begins with a strong rhythm and a clear, end-stopped, rhyme scheme. How does this affect our impression of the speaker's father?

2 Why do you think some of the later rhymes are internal (for instance "skin" and "pin" or "ear" and "year")?

3 The father in the poem does not seem to be aware of the homosexual connotations of earrings, but even in the 1970s using the word "queer" was either old-fashioned or insulting. What does the father's choice of words show about his sensitivity to the modern trend?

4 What joke is Armitage making in his use of the word "nerve" in the second stanza?

5 Comment on Armitage's use of a single sentence to describe how his ear piercing progressed in stanza 2.

6 Explain how the speaker's voice might break "like a tear".

7 Where does the water for the tear come from and what does it represent?

8 The speaker says that the words in italics at the end of the poem are his own, but who do they really belong to?

Themes

The poem describes an attempt at youthful rebellion. It seems to have worked in terms of upsetting the father, but the speaker is less sure about the success of his gesture. He has gained an earring, but not in the properly approved fashion. Later the speaker seems to agree with his father's point of view. Armitage seems to be playing with the idea that for teenagers being an individual sometimes means behaving in the same way as everyone else.

Homecoming

Think, two things on their own and both at once.
The first, that exercise in trust, where those in front
stand with their arms spread wide and free-fall
backwards, blind, and those behind take all the weight.

5 The second, one canary-yellow cotton jacket
on a cloakroom floor, uncoupled from its hook,
becoming scuffed and blackened underfoot. Back home
the very model of a model of a mother, yours, puts
two and two together, makes a proper fist of it
10 and points the finger. Temper, temper. Questions
in the house. You seeing red. Blue murder. Bed.

Then midnight when you slip the latch and sneak
no further than the call-box at the corner of the street;
I'm waiting by the phone, although it doesn't ring
15 because it's sixteen years or so before we'll meet.
Retrace that walk towards the garden gate; in silhouette
a father figure waits there, wants to set things straight.

These ribs are pleats or seams. These arms are sleeves.
These fingertips are buttons, or these hands can fold
20 into a clasp, or else these fingers make a zip
or buckle, you say which. Step backwards into it
and try the same canary-yellow cotton jacket, there,
like this, for size again. It still fits.

Reading for meaning

1 Explain, with diagrams if you wish, the "trust" game that is described in the first stanza.

2 How did the canary-yellow jacket get dirty?

3 Was the "model of a mother" right to assume that the child was to blame?

4 What happened as a consequence of the mother's accusation?

5 What does the child attempt to do after being sent to bed? How far does she go?

6 Who do you think the "I" figure in the poem is?

7 Do you think the "father figure" was actually present at the time of the incident?

8 What does the "I" figure offer the child (now grown up) at the end of the poem?

Literary techniques

1 The poem makes interesting use of time. Identify when each part of the poem is actually taking place.

2 Which moment in the poem seems to be out of its proper time frame? What is the effect of this use of anachronism?

3 The poem uses symbolism to communicate its main idea. In the first stanza, what does being able to lean back show about the relationship between the people involved?

4 In the final stanza, what does the speaker's body become for the loved one?

5 How are the attitudes shown in the first and last stanza related?

6 In the central section, what does the yellow jacket represent in terms of the relationship between the parents and their child?

7 What is the speaker trying to do by "becoming" the yellow jacket?

8 The speaker uses a number of verbs in the imperative (or command) form. What effect does this have on the way we read the poem?

9 Generally the poem has a regular rhythm, but this is disrupted at the end of the second stanza. Why do you think this Simon Armitage has done this?

10 What kind of language is being used at this point in the poem?

Themes

"Homecoming" is a love poem in which a lover attempts to comfort his partner (assuming the speaker is male) about an event that happened in the partner's past. The cause of the partner's unhappiness is a soiled jacket that leads to an argument with her parents. Neither the parents nor the jacket are available now, and so the lover attempts to become both. He is the father figure who holds his daughter in his arms and he is also the jacket that caused the trouble in the first place. The idea of love and trust are central to the poem, as is a desire to make good the mistakes of the past.

November

We walk to the ward from the badly parked car
with your grandma taking four short steps to our two.
We have brought her here to die and we know it.

You check her towel, soap and family trinkets,
5 pare her nails, parcel her in the rough blankets
and she sinks down into her incontinence.

It is time John. In their pasty bloodless smiles,
in their slack breasts, their stunned brains and their baldness,
and in us John: we are almost these monsters.

10 You're shattered. You give me the keys and I drive
through the twilight zone, past the famous station
to your house, to numb ourselves with alcohol.

Inside, we feel the terror of the dusk begin.
Outside we watch the evening, failing again,
15 and we let it happen. We can say nothing.

Sometimes the sun spangles and we feel alive.
One thing we have to get, John, out of this life.

Reading for meaning

1 Who do you think is the speaker in this poem?

2 Using evidence from the first two stanzas, describe the condition of John's grandma.

3 How do you think John feels about his grandma?

4 Suggest two meanings for the sentence "It is time John" at the beginning of stanza 3.

5 What effect does seeing the other old people have on John and the speaker?

6 In what way is the dusk terrifying for the two people in the poem?

7 How would you describe the feelings of the two people as they "watch the evening"?

8 In what sense is the evening "failing"? Or does this word apply to the watchers?

9 What are the two possible readings of the final line?

Simon Armitage

Literary techniques

Armitage pays close attention to rhyme, rhythm and sound effects in this apparently informal poem.

1 What effect is created by the harsh "a" sounds in the first line?

2 What contrast is he pointing out when he rhymes "trinkets" and "blankets" in stanza 2?

3 What is suggested by the tightening of the rhyming in the last five lines of the poem?

4 How does the rhythm of the penultimate line contrast with that of the last one? Why do you think this is?

The imagery in the last part of the poem is extended. It begins with a reference to "twilight" and then continues in the next stanza with the descriptions of the "terror of the dusk" and the evening "failing".

5 What connection is Armitage making between twilight and human lifespan?

6 How does Armitage's allusion to the *Twilight Zone* add to the mystery and threat of this section?

7 How do you think the description of the old people as "monsters" fits into this set of ideas?

8 How are the references to the twilight of the day linked to the title of the poem?

9 Armitage makes creative use of ambiguity on two occasions in the poem. In both instances a seemingly ordinary phrase can be seen to have profound secondary meaning. Why do you think Armitage places these deeper meanings in such ordinary contexts?

Themes

In this poem Armitage approaches the mysteries of old age and death in the most mundane and unglamorous circumstances. John clearly cares for his grandma but he also recognises that her death is inevitable. He is upset as much by thoughts of his own mortality as by her impending death. His companion voices his fears in an attempt to confront them.

Kid

Batman, big shot, when you gave the order
to grow up, then let me loose to wander
leeward, freely through the wild blue yonder
as you liked to say, or ditched me, rather,
5 in the gutter ... well, I turned the corner.
Now I've scotched that "he was like a father
to me" rumour, sacked it, blown the cover
on that "he was like an elder brother"
story, let the cat out on that caper
10 with the married woman, how you took her
downtown on expenses in the motor.
Holy robin-redbreast-nest-egg-shocker!
Holy roll-me-over-in-the-clover,
I'm not playing ball boy any longer
15 Batman, now I've doffed that off-the-shoulder
Sherwood-Forest-green and scarlet number
for a pair of jeans and crew-neck jumper;
now I'm taller, harder, stronger, older.
Batman, it makes a marvellous picture:
20 you without a shadow, stewing over
chicken giblets in the pressure cooker,
next to nothing in the walk-in larder,
punching the palm of your hand all winter,
you baby, now I'm the real boy wonder.

The characters of Batman and Robin first appeared in American comic strips, but they have been portrayed many times on film and on television. This poem seems to be referring to the 1960s television version of Batman. In this version Robin frequently used expressions such as "Holy broken bones, Batman!" and Batman often punched the palm of his hand for emphasis.

Reading for meaning

1 How did Batman see his parting from Robin?

2 How did Robin see this event?

3 How did other people see the relationship between Batman and Robin?

4 How has Robin betrayed Batman?

5 What "crimes" did Batman commit?

6 Briefly describe Robin as he is now.

7 What is Batman's life like?

Literary techniques

1 The poem makes use of contrasting views of the world. Identify the three different points of view in the poem.

2 Contrast Batman and Robin's expressions about the end of their partnership. What do the different word choices show about attitude and audience?

3 What is the effect of Robin's use of colloquial expressions? Why do you think Simon Armitage has used mostly British slang?

4 What impression is created by the two lines beginning with the words "Holy"?

5 What does the phrase "without a shadow" mean in this context?

6 The poem uses the same unstressed rhyme throughout. Where else do you often find this kind of rhyme scheme? What effect does this have?

Themes

This comic poem about comic book characters is a reflection on youth and age. Robin, the Boy Wonder, is now fully grown, while his mentor, Batman, has descended into a feeble and lonely old age. The poem attacks the wholesome and comfortable relationship between the two characters that the 1960s television series showed. Instead of this there are scandals and internal squabbles that show the meanness of both characters. The poem suggests that even super-heroes are only human.

from Book of Matches

Those bastards in their mansions:
to hear them shriek, you'd think
I'd poisoned the dogs and vaulted the ditches,
crossed the lawns in stocking feet and threadbare britches,
5 forced the door of one of the porches, and lifted
the gift of fire from the burning torches,

then given heat and light to streets and houses,
told the people how to ditch their cuffs and shackles,
armed them with the iron from their wrists and ankles.

10 Those lords and ladies in their palaces and castles,
They'd have me sniffed out by their beagles,
picked at by their eagles, pinned down, grilled
beneath the sun.

Me, I stick to the shadows, carry a gun.

Simon Armitage

Reading for meaning

1 How do the rich people seem to feel about the speaker?

2 How big a crime does he seem to have committed?

3 Is there any evidence that a crime has been committed at all?

4 What precautions does the speaker take against the vengeance of the rich?

5 The poem's setting is as ambiguous as the nature of the speaker's crime. When were britches worn and torches used for lighting?

6 With whom do you think the sport of beagling might have been popular?

7 When did rich people live in "palaces and castles"?

Literary techniques

1 This poem partly depends on an *allusion* or indirect reference to the myth of Prometheus. What are the similarities between the speaker's imagined crime and that of Prometheus?

2 The original Prometheus simply gave men the gift of fire. What does the modern version seem to have done as well?

3 Would you describe this poem as a sonnet? Why do you think some of the rhymes are internal (for instance "porches" and "torches" or "beagles" and "eagles")?

The poem is very mysterious. The rich people seem to hate the speaker, but we are not told what he has done to deserve their anger. Instead we are told about the crime that might have cause such a reaction ("You'd think I'd ...").

4 Does this ambiguity make the speaker more or less glamorous? Explain your reasons.

5 What is the effect of the sentence structure in lines 11–13?

6 What is the effect of the single line at the end of the poem?

Themes

The poem updates the Prometheus myth to a more modern setting, though not to the present day. Instead of a myth about defiance of the gods we are offered a story about class struggle set (probably) during the early years of the Industrial Revolution. The speaker of the poem has not actually committed the crimes of stealing fire and educating the people, but he is treated as if he had. The message seems to be that the class struggle is timeless and that those who engage in it need to be cautious.

from Book of Matches

I've made out a will; I'm leaving myself
to the National Health. I'm sure they can use
the jellies and tubes and syrups and glues,
the web of nerves and veins, the loaf of brains,
5 and assortment of fillings and stitches and wounds,
blood – a gallon exactly of bilberry soup –
the chassis or cage or cathedral of bone;
but not the heart, they can leave that alone.

They can have the lot, the whole stock:
10 the loops and coils and sprockets and springs and rods
the twines and cords and strands,
the face, the case, the cogs and the hands,

but not the pendulum, the ticker;
leave that where it stops or hangs.

Reading for meaning

1 What is the speaker leaving to the National Health?

2 What is he excluding from his bequest?

Literary techniques

1 The first two stanzas of the poem use a series of images to describe the speaker's body. What is suggested by each of the following image groups:
   - jellies, tubes, syrups and glues
   - the web of nerves and veins
   - the loaf of brains
   - fillings and stitches and wounds
   - a gallon exactly of bilberry soup
   - the chassis or cage or cathedral of bone?

2 What extended image does the speaker use in the second stanza?

3 The poem has fourteen lines – would you therefore describe it as a sonnet?

4 What are the two possible meanings of "hangs" in the final line of the poem?

Themes

This poem is does not treat its subject – human frailty – very seriously. The first part of the poem looks at the components of a body as if they were spare parts or by-products that could be used beyond the body as "tubes", a "web", "soup" and so on. The clock imagery in the second part of the poem reinforces the idea of our bodies as machines with interchangeable parts. The poem does not talk of the real use of body parts in organ transplants. In excepting the heart from his donation the speaker seems to be saying that the centre of ourselves, our heart or soul, cannot be recycled or given away.

Very little of the imagery in the poem is new or original, but this is part of Armitage's point. We have always made metaphors about our bodies and sometimes we even have several to choose from, for example, "the chassis or cage or cathedral of bone".

Hitcher

I'd been tired, under
the weather, but the ansaphone kept screaming:
One more sick-note, mister, and you're finished. Fired.
I thumbed a lift to where the car was parked.
5 A Vauxhall Astra. It was hired.

I picked him up in Leeds.
He was following the sun to west from east
with just a toothbrush and the good earth for a bed. The truth,
he said, was blowin' in the wind,
10 or round the next bend.

I let him have it
on the top road out of Harrogate – once
with the head, then six times with the krooklok
in the face – and didn't even swerve.
15 I dropped it into third

and leant across
to let him out, and saw him in the mirror
bouncing off the kerb, then disappearing down the verge.
We were the same age, give or take a week.
20 He'd said he liked the breeze

to run its fingers
through his hair. It was twelve noon.
The outlook for the day was moderate to fair.
Stitch that, I remember thinking,
25 you can walk from there.

Reading for meaning

1 How does the speaker feel at the start of the poem?

2 Why does he go to work?

3 Why does the speaker hitch-hike?

4 What reason does the hitcher that the speaker picks up give for travelling?

5 Explain as fully as you can why the speaker attacks the hitcher.

6 What does the fact that the speaker "didn't even swerve" show about his attack?

7 What is the significance of the fact that the hitcher and the speaker are the same age?

8 What does the phrase "stitch that" mean?

9 When would a driver normally use the phrase "you can walk from there"?

10 What does the speaker's lack of emotional response tell us about him?

Literary techniques

1 What is unusual about Armitage's use of rhyme in the first and last stanzas? Why do you think these two stanzas have a consistent rhyme scheme when the others don't?

2 The poem makes interesting use of weather imagery. How does the speaker refer to the weather in the first stanza?

3 What aspect of the weather is the hitcher associated with?

4 What changes in the speaker's view of the weather between the first and last stanzas?

5 As well as the weather the poem frequently mentions quite specific details of the journey and the events that take place.
   • What is the effect of using brand names and place names in the poem?
   • How does this contrast with the event described?

6 The hitcher's life is clearly in contrast with the speaker's, but the figure of the hitcher is not presented simply. Look closely at stanza 2. What impression is created of the hitcher's character?

7 What does his use of an outworn phrase from the 1960s (blowin' in the wind) suggest?

Themes

At first sight this poem contrasts freedom and responsibility. The two young men in the poem are the same age, but one is burdened down by a job while the other is free to follow the sun. The contrast is less obvious on closer examination; the speaker doesn't seem to gain a great deal from his job – he doesn't even own a car; while the freedom of the hitcher seems to be rather undirected and expressed in clichés.

What is clear is that the murder (or at least very serious assault) is the result of a moment of rage at the difference between the two lives. The dead life of the driver is emphasised by his lack of emotional response to his crime.

Ben Jonson

Author profile

Ben Jonson (1572–1637) was a poet and playwright who lived and worked at about the same time as William Shakespeare. This poem reflects on the death of his seven-year-old son. Jonson was writing in a period when religious faith was very strong and when it was believed that innocent, baptised children would go straight to heaven.

On My First Sonne

Farewell, thou child of my right hand, and joy;
My sinne was too much hope of thee, lov'd boy,
Seven yeeres tho'wert lent to me, and I thee pay,
Exacted by thy fate, on the just day.
5 O, could I loose all father, now. For why
Will man lament the state he should envie?
To have so soone scap'd worlds, and fleshes rage,
And, if no other miserie, yet age?
Rest in soft peace, and, ask'd, say here doth lye
10 Ben. Jonson his best piece of poetrie.
For whose sake, hence-forth, all his vowes be such,
As what he loves may never like too much.

1616

Reading for meaning

1 Explain why Jonson describes his son as "child of my right hand".

2 In what way can it be a sin to love someone?

3 Who lent Jonson's son to him?

4 Why should Jonson envy his son?

5 How does Jonson resolve to change after his experience with his son?

Literary techniques

1 Lines 3 and 4 contain an extended metaphor. The original idea is that Ben Jonson's son was lent to him by god or fate and that the debt was reclaimed, "exacted" on the appropriate day.

   - What attitude to God does this metaphor imply? What attitude to earthly joys and possessions does it show?

   - The idea of the things of this world being "lent" to us is explored in the New Testament parable of the talents, which would have been well known to Jonson's audience. What do you think Jonson's use of the word "exacted" shows about the debt collector?

   - Line 5 seems to imply that although he has paid his debt there is still a problem. What would you say the problem was? How does his use of "O" and the word "now" at the end of this sentence help to communicate his emotion?

2 Comment on Jonson's use of alliteration in line 7. How is the poet presenting adult life here?

3 Most of the poem uses single- or two-syllable words which produce a steady and dignified rhythm.

   - Why do you think he uses the three-syllable word "miserie" in the line "And, if no other miserie, yet age?" What effect does this use of "miserie" have on the final two words of the line?

   - How does line 10 make use of a similar technique?

4 The meaning of line 9 is clear but it is highly contracted. Explain who might be doing the asking and who might reply.

5 How does Ben Jonson use rhyme and rhythm to achieve an emphatic ending to his poem?

6 With a partner discuss whether you find the hard-heartedness that the poem recommends convincing. Do you think Jonson intends to follow his own advice?

Key Terms

Extended metaphor – A metaphor is a comparison which states that one thing *is* another, for instance "He is a pig." If the metaphor is elaborated in any way it is said to be **extended**. E.g. "He is a pig, he's always got his snout in the trough."

Themes

The death of a child today is a rare and deeply sad event, but in the past it was very common. Infant mortality rates were high and parents had to prepare themselves mentally for the possible loss of their children. One way of doing this was not to grow too fond of them. Ben Jonson seems to accept these ideas on an intellectual level but the poem indicates that he finds accepting them emotionally slightly more difficult. On the one hand, he says that the child is happy in heaven and that he has avoided most of life's miseries, but on the other this was the child of his right hand, his favourite and "his be.st piece of poetrie". It is not so much losing the child as losing his fatherly feelings that seems to be the problem. In the final part of the poem he resolves to accept conventional wisdom about being a parent.

William Butler Yeats

Author profile

William Butler Yeats was an Irish poet and playwright whose work spanned the end of the 19th century and the beginning of the 20th. He often treated themes to do with life in Ireland or the life of the Irish people. In this poem he assumes the persona of an Irish peasant woman and contrasts her life with that of young people.

The Song of the Old Mother

I rise in the dawn, and I kneel and blow
Till the seed of the fire flicker and glow;
And then I must scrub and bake and sweep
Till stars are beginning to blink and peep;
5 And the young lie long and dream in their bed
Of the matching of ribbons for bosom and head,
And their day goes over in idleness,
And they sigh if the wind but lift a tress:
While I must work because I am old,
10 And the seed of the fire gets feeble and cold.

1899

BACKGROUND

Before matches were readily available, making a fire was a complicated and tedious task. Most people preferred to keep their fires burning continuously, and so the first task of the day was to coax the previous night's fire back to life.

Reading for meaning

1 This poem falls into three sections. Identify these and say what each section contains.

2 What three sources of light is the old mother associated with?

3 What are the main concerns of the young?

4 In the final line do you think the old mother is referring to a real fire?

Literary techniques

1 The poem is written as a single sentence. Comment on the different uses Yeats makes of the word "and" throughout the poem. Do you think the final line refers simply to the old mother or does it also apply to the young?

2 The word "fire" is used twice in the poem. On both occasions Yeats uses alliteration ("flicker" and "feeble"). What do these two terms imply about the fire? What other word does Yeats use to emphasise this quality?

3 The old mother is associated with three sources of light. What do all these sources of light have in common?

4 In contrast with the old mother the young live a life of idleness. How does Yeats use alliteration and internal rhyme in line 5 to emphasise this?

5 What sex are the young people that the old mother seems to be criticising? How can you tell?

6 What quality of light are the young associated with?

7 How does the old woman make fun of young people in line 8?

8 Yeats's choice of words is deliberately simple and basic. What effect does this have on the poem as a whole?

Themes

The contrast between youth and age is a common theme in poetry and one that seems to have fascinated William Butler Yeats. Here the simple and basic language and almost abstract use of ideas like fire, stars and wind gives the poem a universal and timeless appeal. The old mother "must work" because she is old, but in contrasting her own life with that of idle young women she does not seem particularly resentful. After all, she was young once and the young will one day be old themselves.

William Wordsworth

Author profile

William Wordsworth (1770–1850) was born and
brought up in the Lake District. When he began
writing poetry he felt that it should reflect the lives
and the language of ordinary people. In this poem
he imagines the feelings of a woman who has not
seen her son for seven years.

The Affliction of Margaret

Where art thou, my beloved Son,
Where art thou, worse to me than dead?
Oh find me, prosperous or undone!
Or, if the grave be now thy bed,
5 Why am I ignorant of the same
That I may rest; and neither blame,
Nor sorrow may attend thy name?

Seven years, alas! to have received
No tidings of an only child;
10 To have despaired, and have believed,
And be for evermore beguiled;
Sometimes with thoughts of very bliss!
I catch at them, and then I miss;
Was ever darkness like to this?

15 He was among the prime in worth,
An object beauteous to behold;
Well born, well bred; I sent him forth
Ingenuous, innocent, and bold:
If things ensued that wanted grace,
20 As hath been said, they were not base;
And never blush was on my face.

Ah! little doth the Young One dream,
When full of play and childish cares,
What power hath even his wildest scream,
25 Heard by his Mother unawares!
He knows it not, he cannot guess:
Years to a Mother bring distress;
But do not make her love the less.

Neglect me! no, I suffered long
30 From that ill thought; and, being blind,
Said, "Pride shall help me in my wrong;
Kind mother have I been, as kind
As ever breathed:" and that is true;
I've wet my path with tears like dew,
35 Weeping for him when no one knew.

My Son, if thou be humbled, poor,
Hopeless of honour and of gain,
Oh! do not dread thy mother's door;
Think not of me with grief and pain:
40 I now can see with better eyes;
And worldly grandeur I despise,
And fortune with her gifts and lies.

Alas! the fowls of Heaven have wings,
And blasts of Heaven will aid their flight;
45 They mount – how short a voyage brings
The Wanderers back to their delight!
Chains tie us down by land and sea;
And wishes, vain as mine, may be
All that is left to comfort thee.

50 Perhaps some dungeon hears thee groan,
Maimed, mangled by inhuman men;
Or thou upon a Desart thrown
Inheritest the Lion's Den;
Or hast been summon'd to the Deep,
55 Thou, Thou, and all thy mates, to keep
An incommunicable sleep.

I look for Ghosts; but none will force
Their way to me: 'tis falsely said
That there was ever intercourse
60 Between the living and the dead;
For, surely, then I should have sight
Of Him I wait for day and night,
With love and longings infinite.

My apprehensions come in crowds;
65 I dread the rustling of the grass;
The very shadows of the clouds
Have power to shake me as they pass;
I question things, and do not find
One that will answer to my mind;
70 And all the world appears unkind.

Beyond participation lie
My troubles, and beyond relief:
If any chance to heave a sigh
They pity me, and not my grief.
75 Then come to me, my Son, or send
Some tidings that my woes may end;
I have no other earthly friend.

1807

Reading for meaning

1 What does Margaret imagine might have happened to her son?

2 Why is she so upset about not hearing from him for seven years?

3 What was Margaret's son like when he set out from home?

4 According to the poem, what power do all young people have over their parents?

5 Why does Margaret not feel that her son might be deliberately neglecting her?

6 What explanations for his non-appearance does she suggest?

7 How does the lack of news from her son make her feel?

Literary techniques

1 This poem has a very regular rhyme scheme. What is it?

2 It also uses mostly end-stopped lines. What is the effect of this on the way the poem sounds?

3 In spite of the strong rhyme scheme, how does Wordsworth attempt to make the poem seem like a woman speaking?

4 How does Wordsworth use alliteration to express Margaret's pride in her son in the third stanza?

5 How do lines 64 to 70 express the completeness of Margaret's unhappiness?

6 How does assonance help to make the last line more poignant?

Themes

The theme of this poem is a mother's love for her child, but its choice of a quite ordinary mother was unusual for its time. The situation it describes was a common one in the early 19th century. People often had to leave home to find work and communication with those left behind was not easy. We are given no clue about why Margaret's son has not been in touch and she explores all her worst fears in an attempt explain his silence. The one thing she won't accept is that his neglect is due to lack of love for her.

William Blake

Author profile

William Blake (1757–1827), a prolific poet and painter, wrote at a time when attitudes to children were changing. At the end of the 18th century children were simply regarded as small adults and childhood was not seen as anything special. Blake's *Songs of Innocence* and *Songs of Experience* drew attention to the innocence and vulnerability of children. Blake was a deeply religious writer and much of his poetry draws on Biblical and religious ideas.

The Little Boy Lost

'Father, father, where are you going?
O do not walk so fast!
Speak, father, speak to your little boy
Or else I shall be lost.'

5 The night was dark, no father was there,
The child was wet with dew;
The mire was deep, and the child did weep,
And away the vapour flew.

1789

Reading for meaning

1 Explain as fully as you can how the little boy came to be lost.

Literary techniques

1 How does Blake make the boy's situation more dramatic in the first stanza?

2 The second stanza consists of a series of simple sentences. How are these used to emphasise the boy's plight?

3 Why do you think the poem ends with the disappearance of the vapour rather than the disappearance of the father? What would the boy have known at this point?

The Little Boy Found

The little boy lost in the lonely fen,
Led by the wand'ring light,
Began to cry; but God, ever nigh,
Appeared like his father in white.

5 He kissed the child, and by the hand led,
And to his mother brought,
Who in sorrow pale, through the lonely dale
Her little boy weeping sought.

1789

BACKGROUND

The "wandering light" would be a "will-o'-the-wisp", a pale light caused by the spontaneous combustion of marsh gases. Blake's readers would also have been aware that the Children of Israel were led through the Wilderness at night by a column of light provided by God.

Reading for meaning

1 What part does God play in rescuing the boy?

2 Do you think the word "weeping" in the final line applies to the mother, the boy or both?

Literary techniques

1 What kind of audience do these poems seem to have been written for? Consider their use of very simple language, short lines, a clear rhyme scheme and the fact that God intervenes directly in the second poem.

2 How does Blake use alliteration in the first two lines of this poem to emphasise the boy's isolation?

3 How are the roles of God and that of a father connected?

Themes

These two poems are taken from *Songs of Innocence*, a series of poems that were either addressed to children or which took a child's point of view. The first poem plays on children's fears of being abandoned, while the second provides reassurance to children that God will intervene in their troubles. For adult readers, however, a symbolic reading of the poem is possible. The child stands for any human being lost in the world. Our only hope of rescue is if we recognise our true father; that is, God.

Chidiock Tichborne

Chidiock Tichborne (?1558–86) was one of the Forty Roman Catholic Martyrs of England and Wales who died in the religious persecutions of the 16th century. As the subtitle informs us, this poem was written in the Tower of London shortly before Tichborne's execution. The elegy expresses its ideas simply but with some force.

Tichborne was hanged and, in the words of a contemporary, "they were all cut down, their privities were cut off, bowelled alive and seeing, and quartered".

Tichborne's Elegy

Written with his own hand in the Tower before his execution

My prime of youth is but a frost of cares,
My feast of joy is but a dish of pain,
My crop of corn is but a field of tares,
And all my good is but vain hope of gain.
5 The day is past, and yet I saw no sun;
And now I live, and now my life is done.

My tale was heard, and yet it was not told,
My fruit is fallen, and yet my leaves are green;
My youth is spent, and yet I am not old,
10 I saw the world, and yet I was not seen.
My thread is cut, and yet it is not spun;
And now I live, and now my life is done.

I sought my death, and found it in my womb,
I looked for life and saw it was a shade;
15 I trod the earth, and knew it was my tomb,
And now I die, and now I was but made.
My glass is full, and now my glass is run;
And now I live, and now my life is done.

1586

Key Terms

Elegy – a mournful or plaintive poem – usually a lament for the dead. Obviously very few poets had the opportunity to write their own elegies.

Reading for meaning

1 The first stanza deals with expectations and disappointments. Make a list of each.

2 The second stanza expresses Tichborne's situation as a series or paradoxes. What are they?

3 The third stanza points out that, for Tichborne, extremes such as birth and death are virtually the same thing. Each stanza ends with the refrain "And now I live, and now my life is done." With a partner discuss whether you think all the contrasts in the poem work equally well. Is there one contrast you find particularly effective?

4 Do you think Tichborne offers any interesting or original contrasts or do most of them seem quite conventional?

5 Would you view the poem differently if its author had not been executed immediately after writing it?

Literary techniques

1 How does using the same structure for each set of statements help to make the poem more emphatic?

2 Why do you think Tichborne chose to end each stanza with a refrain?

3 Why do you think Tichborne used the line "And now I die, and now I was but made" towards the end of the poem?

4 The first three lines of stanzas 1 and 2 begin with "My", whereas the first three lines of stanza 3 begin with "I". Why do you think Tichborne broke the pattern he had established at this point?

Themes

"Tichborne's Elegy" is a curiously earthbound poem for someone who believed he was about to meet his maker. It looks chiefly at the enforced brevity of the poet's life. He was twenty-eight years old.

Thomas Hardy

Author profile

Thomas Hardy (1840–1928) is famous as a
19th-century novelist and a 20th-century poet.
In this poem he uses the persona of an
ordinary soldier to reflect on the ironies of war.
It was written when the British army was
fighting the Second Boer War in South Africa,
but the situation it describes is true of almost
any war anywhere.

The Man He Killed

"Had he and I but met
   By some old ancient inn,
We should have sat us down to wet
   Right many a nipperkin!

5 "But ranged as infantry,
   And staring face to face,
I shot at him as he at me,
   And killed him in his place.

"I shot him dead because —
10   Because he was my foe,
Just so: my foe of course he was;
   That's clear enough; although

"He thought he'd 'list, perhaps,
   Off-hand like — just as I —
15 Was out of work — had sold his traps —
   No other reason why.

"Yes; quaint and curious war is!
   You shoot a fellow down
You'd treat if met where any bar is,
20   Or help to half-a-crown."

1902

BACKGROUND

Half-a-crown – twelve and a half pence, but the modern equivalent would probably be "a tenner".

Nipperkin – a small wine or beer measure. Now called a "nip".

Reading for meaning

1 How would the soldier have treated the man he killed if they had met socially?

2 What do you think the speaker did before he enlisted?

3 Why do you think he enlisted?

4 What do you think the soldier means when he describes war as "quaint and curious"?

Literary techniques

1 Hardy uses a number of colloquial expressions in this poem. With a partner identify them and make sure you know what they mean.

2 What impression do you gain of the soldier from his use of the words "old ancient" to describe the inn?

3 The third stanza of this poem seems to be crowded with sound effects and other devices and deserves a careful reading.

   • Why do you think the word "because" is repeated?

   • What is the effect of so many words that rhyme with "foe" in this stanza?

   • Why do you think the stanza runs on into the next instead of being end stopped like the others?

   • Explain as fully as you can why Hardy has placed so much emphasis on stanza 3.

4 Why are there so many pauses – indicated by dashes – in the fourth stanza? What is the soldier beginning to understand at this point?

5 What does the soldier's imagined life of his foe reveal to the reader?

6 Why do you think Hardy chose to rhyme "war is" and "bar is" in the final stanza? What point is he making here?

7 What do you think is Hardy's attitude to war? Point to evidence in the poem to support your answer.

Themes

The speaker in the poem is a killer, but unlike many in this anthology, he has killed at the command of others rather than for personal motives. The poem reveals that the soldier has enlisted through economic necessity and that he has killed a man who in other circumstances could have been a companion. The soldier himself is only able to describe his experience as "quaint and curious", but the situation described by Hardy might prompt the reader to reflect on the senselessness of war and the way it distorts the lives and values of those involved.

Walt Whitman

Author profile

Walt Whitman (1819–92) was an American poet who celebrated the many elements that make up democracy and who revelled in simple existence. Barnegat Bay is at the north end of Long Beach Island, New Jersey; at the time this poem was written, it was known as a dangerous and unpredictable sea passage.

Patrolling Barnegat

Wild, wild the storm, and the sea high running,
Steady the roar of the gale, with incessant undertone muttering,
Shouts of demoniac laughter fitfully piercing and pealing,
Waves, air, midnight, their savagest trinity lashing,
5 Out in the shadows there milk-white coombs careering,
On beachy slush and sand spirits of snow fierce slanting,
Where through the murk the easterly death-wind breasting,
Through cutting swirl and spray watchful firm advancing,
(That in the distance! is that a wreck? is the red signal flaring?)
10 Slush and sand of the beach tireless till daylight wending,
Steadily, slowly, through hoarse roar never remitting,
Along the midnight edge by those milk-white coombs careering,
A group of dim, weird forms, struggling, the night confronting,
That savage trinity warily watching.

1880

Reading for meaning

1 What do you think is the cause of the "shouts of demoniac laughter"?

2 Who are the "savage trinity"?

3 What do the "milk-white combs" indicate?

4 What elements of the description tell us that it is winter?

5 In what sense is the easterly wind a "death-wind"?

6 At what point in the poem are the activities of the patrollers introduced?

7 What are the "dim, weird forms"? Why do you think they are named at such a late point in a poem called "Patrolling Barnegat"?

Literary techniques

1 Almost all the verbs in this poem are in the continuous present tense (ending in "-ing"). What is the effect of this?

2 What is the effect of placing most of the verbs at the end of the lines?

3 Which verbs do not end in "-ing"? What ideas do they express?

4 What effect does Whitman achieve by using the words "roar", "muttering" and "shouts of demoniac laughter ... pealing" in lines 2 and 3? Where else might you hear a similar variety of sounds?

5 Comment on the effect of the alliteration in line 6.

6 Look at the verbs that are applied to the patrollers. What ideas do these verbs express?

7 The last line of the poem is ambiguous. Who is doing the watching? The patrollers? The "savage trinity"? Or both?

8 This poem has fourteen lines and is divided into a sestet and an octave; it has a rather simple rhyme scheme but it conforms to most definitions of a sonnet. Which rule of the sonnet form does "Patrolling Barnegat" break most obviously? Can you suggest why?

Themes

In this poem Walt Whitman attempts to express the power of a storm in winter. Against the power of "waves, air" and "midnight" are posed the "weird, dim forms" of the human beings. Their purpose, to watch for wrecks, is made incredibly difficult by the darkness and storm, so that they struggle to do such simple things as walk along the beach. They barely have a place in this savage environment.

William Shakespeare

William Shakespeare (1564–1616) wrote a series of 153 sonnets addressed to a young man and a young woman which were published, in mysterious circumstances, in 1609. The sonnet was a very popular form at this time and was frequently used to express love. In this sonnet Shakespeare expresses his love for a woman known to history as "the dark lady".

Sonnet 130

My mistress' eyes are nothing like the sun;
Coral is far more red than her lips' red.
If snow be white, why then her breasts are dun;
If hairs be wires, black wires grow on her head.
5 I have seen roses damasked, red and white,
But no such roses see I in her cheeks;
And in some perfumes is there more delight
Than in the breath that from my mistress reeks.
I love to hear her speak, yet well I know
10 That music hath a far more pleasing sound.
I grant I never saw a goddess go;
My mistress when she walks treads on the ground.
    And yet, by heaven, I think my love as rare
    As any she belied with false compare.

1609

Reading for meaning

1 What, according to the sonnet, is wrong with the following features of his mistress:

- eyes
- lips
- breasts
- cheeks
- breath
- voice
- movement?

2 How does the speaker feel about his mistress?

3 Do you think the dark lady would have been pleased with this poem? Give reasons for your opinion.

4 Judging by what Shakespeare says his mistress is *not* like, what can you tell about the love poetry of this period?

5 Would you say that this poem was mostly about love or mostly about love poetry?

Literary techniques

1 The poem consists of a simple list of the qualities of the poet's beloved. At what point do we realise that it is not a complaint?

2 What kind of imagery does Shakespeare and the other poets of the period seem to have used to reflect human qualities?

3 Where is Shakespeare's strongest expression of affection? How is this reflected in the rhyme scheme?

Themes

Shakespeare's sonnet demonstrates strong affection for his mistress, but he seems more concerned about honesty of expression than making her feel good. In doing so he is criticising other sonnets of the period that exaggerated the beauty of the women they were addressed to without regard to reality. He is also saying that in love, physical perfection is less important than sincerity and genuine affection.

Robert Browning

Author profile

Robert Browning (1812–1889) was one of the most successful poets of the Victorian period. He was particularly interested in exploring psychological aspects of characters and is famous for his use of the dramatic monologue as a means of doing this. The following two poems are part of a series in which Browning explored the characters of murderers.

My Last Duchess

Ferrara

That's my last Duchess painted on the wall,
Looking as if she were alive. I call
That piece a wonder, now: Frà Pandolf's hands
Worked busily a day, and there she stands.
5 Will 't please you sit and look at her? I said
"Frà Pandolf" by design, for never read
Strangers like you that pictured countenance,
The depth and passion of its earnest glance,
But to myself they turned (since none puts by
10 The curtain I have drawn for you, but I)
And seemed as they would ask me, if they durst,
How such a glance came there; so, not the first
Are you to turn and ask thus. Sir, 'twas not
Her husband's presence only, called that spot
15 Of joy into the Duchess' cheek: perhaps
Frà Pandolf chanced to say "Her mantle laps
Over my lady's wrist too much," or "Paint
Must never hope to reproduce the faint
Half-flush that dies along her throat": such stuff
20 Was courtesy, she thought, and cause enough
For calling up that spot of joy. She had
A heart – how shall I say? – too soon made glad,
Too easily impressed; she liked whate'er
She looked on, and her looks went everywhere.
25 Sir, 'twas all one! My favour at her breast,
The dropping of the daylight in the West,
The bough of cherries some officious fool
Broke in the orchard for her, the white mule
She rode with round the terrace — all and each
30 Would draw from her alike the approving speech,
Or blush, at least. She thanked men, — good! but thanked —
Somehow – I know not how – as if she ranked
My gift of a nine-hundred-years-old name

With anybody's gift. Who'd stoop to blame
35 This sort of trifling? Even had you skill
In speech — (which I have not) — to make your will
Quite clear to such a one, and say, "Just this
Or that in you disgusts me; here you miss,
Or there exceed the mark" — and if she let
40 Herself be lessoned so, nor plainly set
Her wits to yours, forsooth, and made excuse,
— E'en then would be some stooping; and I choose
Never to stoop. Oh sir, she smiled, no doubt,
Whene'er I passed her; but who passed without
45 Much the same smile? This grew; I gave commands;
Then all smiles stopped together. There she stands
As if alive. Will 't please you rise? We'll meet
The company below, then. I repeat,
The Count your master's known munificence
50 Is ample warrant that no just pretence
Of mine for dowry will be disallowed;
Though his fair daughter's self, as I avowed
At starting, is my object. Nay, we'll go
Together down, sir. Notice Neptune, though,
55 Taming a sea-horse, thought a rarity,
Which Claus of Innsbruck cast in bronze for me.

1845

Ferrara – this city in Northern Italy was a centre of the Renaissance under the powerful House of Este. At that time Italy was a collection of city states whose rulers were all powerful. Alfonso II, the fifth Duke of Ferrara, and his young first wife, Lucrezia de Medici, have been associated with the poem. The Duke had three wives in all.

Reading for meaning

1 Who painted the portrait of the Duchess?

2 Who is allowed to look at it?

3 Who is the Duke talking to?

4 The Duke mentions some of the things that were inclined to make the Duchess smile.

 • Why did the Duchess's behaviour annoy the Duke?

 • Why didn't he tell her off about it?

 • What did he do instead?

5 How do you think the Duke now regards his wife?

6 With a partner decide whether you think the Duke is mad, or simply extremely arrogant.

Literary techniques

1 This poem is in the form of a dramatic monologue, in which the speaker is the Duke of Ferrara and the implied listener is an ambassador negotiating the Duke's next marriage. Why do you think the ambassador never speaks?

2 Browning has gone to the trouble of writing this poem in rhyming couplets, but readers seldom notice this.

 • What technique has Browning used to make the rhyme scheme less noticeable?

 • How else has he tried to make the poem like a person speaking?

3 Why does the Duke say "all smiles stopped together" rather than something more explicit?

4 The artists Frà Pandolf and Claus of Innsbruck have both been invented by Browning. Why do you think the Duke mentions these names? What do we assume about them?

Key Terms

Dramatic monologue – a technique in which the poet adopts the persona of a particular character and the poem consists of either an address to the reader or to an implied listener.

Themes

This portrait of a murderer is also a portrait of power and prestige. The Duke is so secure in his social, financial and political world that he can talk matter-of-factly about the killing of his wife to a man who has come to negotiate his second marriage. At the same time there is some passion here. The wife who was too readily pleased has now become a treasured possession that the Duke likes to see and show off at his discretion.

English Literature: Poetry

Robert Browning

The Laboratory

ANCIEN RÉGIME

Now that I, tying thy glass mask tightly,
May gaze thro' these faint smokes curling whitely,
As thou pliest thy trade in this devil's-smithy —
Which is the poison to poison her, prithee?

5 He is with her; and they know that I know
Where they are, what they do: they believe my tears flow
While they laugh, laugh at me, at me fled to the drear
Empty church, to pray God in, for them! — I am here.

Grind away, moisten and mash up thy paste,
10 Pound at thy powder, — I am not in haste!
Better sit thus, and observe thy strange things,
Than go where men wait me and dance at the King's.

That in the mortar — you call it a gum?
Ah, the brave tree whence such gold oozings come!
15 And yonder soft phial, the exquisite blue,
Sure to taste sweetly, — is that poison too?

Had I but all of them, thee and thy treasures,
What a wild crowd of invisible pleasures!
To carry pure death in an earring, a casket,
20 A signet, a fan-mount, a filigree-basket!

Soon, at the King's, a mere lozenge to give,
And Pauline should have just thirty minutes to live!
But to light a pastile, and Elise, with her head
And her breast and her arms and her hands, should drop dead!

25 Quick — is it finished? The colour's too grim!
Why not soft like the phial's, enticing and dim?
Let it brighten her drink, let her turn it and stir,
And try it and taste, ere she fix and prefer!

What a drop! She's not little, no minion like me!
30 That's why she ensnared him: this never will free
The soul from those masculine eyes, — say, 'no!'
To that pulse's magnificent come-and-go.

For only last night, as they whispered, I brought
My own eyes to bear on her so, that I thought
35 Could I keep them one half minute fixed, she would
Shrivelled; she fell not; yet this does it all!

Not that I bid you spare her the pain;
Let death be felt and the proof remain:
Brand, burn up, bite into its grace —
40 He is sure to remember her dying face!

Is it done? Take my mask off! Nay, be not morose;
It kills her, and this prevents seeing it close:
The delicate droplet, my whole fortune's fee! —
If it hurts her, beside, can it ever hurt me?

45 Now, take all my jewels, gorge gold to your fill,
You may kiss me, old man, on my mouth if you will!
But brush this dust off me, lest horror it brings
Ere I know it — next moment I dance at the King's!

1845

Reading for meaning

1 Why is the speaker wearing a "glass mask"?

2 Why does the speaker want to purchase some poison?

3 What aspects of the old man's art does the speaker like particularly?

4 Who else does the speaker think of killing? Why?

5 What is the main physical difference between the speaker and her rival? Do you think this difference might have an impact on the way she feels about herself?

6 What sort of death does the speaker want for her rival?

7 How much does the speaker pay for the poison? What does this show about the strength of her feelings?

8 Why do you think the speaker, an aristocrat, allows the old man to kiss her on the lips?

Literary techniques

The final line of the first stanza uses a dactylic rhythm – that is, one stressed syllable followed by two unstressed syllables:

/ ∪ ∪ / ∪ ∪ / ∪ ∪ / ∪
Which is the poison to poison her, prithee?

1 What is the effect of this rather jolly rhythm here? Can you find other examples of its use?

2 How does the poem's clear, end-stopped rhyme scheme contribute to its tone?

3 What is the effect of the alliteration in lines 9 and 10?

4 How does the poem make use of colour?

5 What does the repeated phrase "dance at the King's" suggest about the speaker's social life and social position?

6 What does the alliteration in line 39 suggest about the intensity of the speaker's feelings?

Themes

Browning's portrait of a murderess is very different from that of the murderer in "My Last Duchess". Both killers have wealth and status, but the speaker in "The Laboratory" must use stealth and lose her wealth and some of her status to achieve her ends. Her motives are sexual jealousy and insecurity and she displays a certain cruel relish at the prospect of her rival's death.

Alfred Tennyson

Author profile

Alfred Tennyson (1809–1892) was Queen Victoria's favourite poet; he was appointed Poet Laureate in 1850. His poetry often took its inspiration from literary sources; in this poem he uses the dramatic monologue to take on the persona of the famous Greek hero king, Ulysses.

Ulysses

It little profits that an idle king,
By this still hearth, among these barren crags,
Matched with an agèd wife, I mete and dole
Unequal laws unto a savage race,
5 That hoard, and sleep, and feed, and know not me.

I cannot rest from travel: I will drink
Life to the lees: all times I have enjoyed
Greatly, have suffered greatly, both with those
That loved me, and alone; on shore, and when
10 Through scudding drifts the rainy Hyades
Vext the dim sea: I am become a name;
For always roaming with a hungry heart
Much have I seen and known; cities of men
And manners, climates, councils, governments,
15 Myself not least, but honoured of them all;
And drunk delight of battle with my peers,
Far on the ringing plains of windy Troy.
I am a part of all that I have met;
Yet all experience is an arch wherethrough
20 Gleams that untravelled world, whose margin fades
For ever and for ever when I move.
How dull it is to pause, to make an end,
To rust unburnished, not to shine in use!
As though to breathe were life. Life piled on life
25 Were all too little, and of one to me
Little remains: but every hour is saved
From that eternal silence, something more,
A bringer of new things; and vile it were
For some three suns to store and hoard myself,
30 And this gray spirit yearning in desire
To follow knowledge like a sinking star,
Beyond the utmost bound of human thought.

This is my son, mine own Telemachus,
To whom I leave the sceptre and the isle —
35 Well-loved of me, discerning to fulfill
This labour, by slow prudence to make mild
A rugged people, and through soft degrees
Subdue them to the useful and the good.
Most blameless is he, centred in the sphere
40 Of common duties, decent not to fail
In offices of tenderness, and pay
Meet adoration to my household gods,
When I am gone. He works his work, I mine.

There lies the port; the vessel puffs her sail:
45 There gloom the dark broad seas. My mariners,
Souls that have toiled, and wrought, and thought with me —
That ever with a frolic welcome took
The thunder and the sunshine, and opposed
Free hearts, free foreheads — you and I are old;
50 Old age hath yet his honour and his toil;
Death closes all: but something ere the end,
Some work of noble note, may yet be done,
Not unbecoming men that strove with Gods.
The lights begin to twinkle from the rocks:
55 The long day wanes: the slow moon climbs: the deep
Moans round with many voices. Come, my friends,
'Tis not too late to seek a newer world.
Push off, and sitting well in order smite
The sounding furrows; for my purpose holds
60 To sail beyond the sunset, and the baths
Of all the western stars, until I die.
It may be that the gulfs will wash us down:
It may be we shall touch the Happy Isles,
And see the great Achilles, whom we knew.
65 Though much is taken, much abides; and though
We are not now that strength which in old days
Moved earth and heaven, that which we are, we are;
One equal temper of heroic hearts,
Made weak by time and fate, but strong in will
70 To strive, to seek, to find, and not to yield.

1842

Reading for meaning

1 How does Ulysses feel about the people he rules?

2 What does the phrase "drink life to the lees" mean? Why do you think this expression is appropriate here?

3 What impression of Ulysses do you get from his description of his former travels?

4 What is making Ulysses unhappy at present?

5 How does Ulysses differ from his son Telemachus?

6 How does Ulysses propose to break his current mood?

7 How would you describe the speaker's mood at the end of the poem?

Literary techniques

This poem is notable for its strong, emphatic rhythms. Line 5 could be scanned:

ᴗ / ᴗ / ᴗ / ᴗ / ᴗ /
That hoard, and sleep, and feed, and know not me.

1 **Mark the final line of the poem in a similar way. What kinds of words are stressed in the two lines? Which line is more emphatic? Why do you think this is?**

Tennyson also achieves emphasis by careful combinations of monosyllabic and polysyllabic words. For instance, the slow monosyllabic line 5 is preceded by the quicker polysyllabic "Unequal laws unto a savage race".

2 **Find other examples where Tennyson uses monosyllabic and polysyllabic lines to vary the pace of his poem.**

3 **How does the run-on between lines 7 and 8 help to give an impression of the nature of Ulysses' earlier life?**

4 **Lines 6 to 17 are a single sentence. The following sentence is four lines long, and the one after that consists of only two lines. What is the effect of this variation in sentence length?**

5 **How does the imagery in the section on Telemachus contrast with the images used in the rest of the poem?**

6 **The final section of the poem is addressed to the mariners. What techniques does Tennyson use to persuade them to join him on his final voyage?**

Themes

Tennyson here presents a vision of an old man who refuses to be bowed by age and infirmity. Ulysses looks back on the pleasures and pains of his youth with satisfaction and pride, but he is determined not give in to old age now that his strength has begun to diminish. He will continue "To strive, to seek, to find, and not to yield".

Oliver Goldsmith

Author profile

Oliver Goldsmith (1730–74) was an Irish poet, dramatist
and novelist. His works include the poem "The
Deserted Village", the comedy *She Stoops to Conquer*
and the novel *The Vicar of Wakefield*. "The Village
Schoolmaster" is an extract from "the Deserted
Village", a description of the depopulation of the
countryside in the latter part of the 18th century.

The Village Schoolmaster

Beside yon straggling fence that skirts the way,
With blossomed furze unprofitably gay,
There, in his mansion, skilled to rule,
The village master taught his little school;
5 A man severe he was, and stern to view,
I knew him well, and every truant knew;
Well had the boding tremblers learned to trace
The day's disasters in his morning face;
Full well they laughed with counterfeited glee,
10 At all his jokes, for many a joke had he:
Full well the busy whisper, circling round,
Conveyed the dismal tidings when he frowned;
Yet he was kind, or, if severe in aught,
The love he bore to learning was in fault;
15 The village all declared how much he knew;
'Twas certain he could write, and cipher too:
Lands he could measure, terms and tides presage,
And even the story ran that he could gauge.
In arguing, too, the person owned his skill,
20 For, even though vanquished, he could argue still;
While words of learned length and thundering sound
Amazed the gazing rustics ranged around;
And still they gazed, and still the wonder grew
That one small head could carry all he knew.

1770

BACKGROUND

Boding – foreboding or worrying.

Cipher – to perform arithmetical calculations.

Gauge – to measure the capacity of a barrel or keg.

Reading for meaning

1 What does the fact that the schoolmaster lived where he taught tell you about the size of his school?

2 Who do you think the "boding tremblers" were?

3 How did the students respond to their teacher?

4 What does this tell you about his methods of discipline?

5 What was the attitude of the villagers to the schoolmaster?

6 What does this tell you about the general level of education at that time?

Literary techniques

1 What is the effect of using rhyming couplets throughout the poem?

2 Goldsmith's choice of words is generally simple. What effect do words and phrases like "boding tremblers", "counterfeited glee", "dismal tidings" and "vanquished" have when used in such a context?

3 How does the sound pattern in the poem change in lines 21–23? Why do you think this is?

4 How does line 24 contrast with the previous three lines? How well does it round off the poem?

Themes

This poem presents the character of a schoolmaster as well as providing an insight into his social and cultural setting. He is feared by his students and respected by adults, while his learning is a subject of wonder to all. Goldsmith does not idealise his subject – who clearly ruled his students through fear – but at least there is some kindness in the man and his main motivation is love of learning.

Alfred Tennyson

The Eagle

He clasps the crag with crookèd hands;
Close to the sun in lonely lands,
Ring'd with the azure world, he stands.

The wrinkled sea beneath him crawls;
5 He watches from his mountain walls,
And like a thunderbolt he falls.

1851

Reading for meaning

1 Where is the eagle?

2 In what way might the world be azure (blue)?

3 How high is the eagle? Quote the evidence for your answer.

4 Why do you think the mountains are described as "walls"?

5 What mythological figure do you associate with a "thunderbolt"?

Literary techniques

1 Why do you think Tennyson uses the word "hands" in line 1 instead of "claws"
or "talons"?

2 In line 3 the eagle is "ring'd with the azure world". What relationship between the
world and the eagle does this line express? What does it tell us about the eagle's point
of view?

3 Why do you think Tennyson describes the sea as "wrinkled"? What does this tell us
about the eagle's point of view?

4 Comment on Tennyson's use of alliteration in this poem.

Themes

Much of the meaning of this poem is conveyed through subtle use of imagery. The loneliness,
power and arrogance of the eagle are all conveyed through Tennyson's description of the
landscape in which it sits.

Gerard Manley Hopkins

Author profile

Gerard Manley Hopkins (1844–89) spent his working life as a Roman Catholic priest, and his major poetry was not published until after his death at the age of 45. His highly original poems looked back to alliterative Anglo-Saxon poetry for inspiration and frequently experimented with unusual rhythms. In describing places he aimed to capture their inner landscape or "inscape" as well as their outward appearance.

Inversnaid

This darksome burn, horseback brown,
His rollrock highroad roaring down,
In coop and in comb the fleece of his foam
Flutes and low to the lake falls home.

5 A windpuff-bonnet of fawn-froth
Turns and twindles over the broth
Of a pool so pitchblack, fell-frowning,
It rounds and rounds Despair to drowning.

Degged with dew, dappled with dew,
10 Are the groins of the braes that the brook treads through,
Wiry heathpacks, flitches of fern,
And the beadbonny ash that sits over the burn.

What would the world be, once bereft
Of wet and wildness? Let them be left,
15 O let them be left, wildness and wet;
Long live the weeds and the wilderness yet.

1881

BACKGROUND

Fell – a mountain of hill, but also fierce and terrible.

Degged – dappled.

Groin – the point where two hillsides join.

Brae – a hill or hillside.

Flitches – literally sides of bacon, but here referring to the long thin hillsides covered in ferns.

Beadbonny – covered in berries.

Reading for meaning

1 How would you describe the speed and power of the burn at the beginning of the poem?

2 What happens when it reaches the valleys?

3 Describe the pool in your own words.

4 What impression of the landscape is created in the third stanza?

5 What is Gerard Manley Hopkins worried about in the fourth stanza?

Literary techniques

1 This poem makes extensive use of alliteration, both as a structuring device and for effect.

   • How is alliteration consistently used to help structure the poem?

   • Discuss any examples in the poem where you find the alliteration particularly effective.

   • Would you say that there is too much alliteration in the poem? Does it make the poem sound unnatural?

2 The word "twindle" is not in most dictionaries. What other words is it similar to? What do you think it means?

3 Why do you think "Despair" is spelt with a capital letter?

4 What animal is suggested in the image of "wiry heathpacks"?

5 What impression of the ash tree do we get when we are told that it "sits" over the stream (the burn)?

6 Explain why there is so much repetition in the final stanza.

Themes

Gerard Manley Hopkins attempts to capture his impression of the natural landscape in this poem. While describing its outward appearance, he is also keen to express its inner beauty, strength and energy. At the end of the poem Hopkins stresses the uniqueness of the valley of Inversnaid and its importance to human beings. Although not useful as farmland or as a place to live, Hopkins suggests that the world needs wet and wild places just as much as more hospitable landscapes.

John Clare

Author profile

John Clare (1793–1864) is famous for his
descriptions of country life, particularly in *The
Shepherd's Calendar* (1827) and *The Rural Muse*
(1835). He was confined in a lunatic asylum from
1837. In this simple sonnet he attempts to capture
the peace and tranquillity of an English summer.

Sonnet

I love to see the summer beaming forth
And white wool sack clouds sailing to the north
I love to see the wild flowers come again
And Mare blobs stain with gold the meadow drain
5 And water lilies whiten on the floods
Where reed clumps rustle like a wind shook wood
Where from her hiding place the Moor Hen pushes
And seeks her flag nest floating in bull rushes
I like the willow leaning half way o'er
10 The clear deep lake to stand upon its shore
I love the hay grass when the flower head swings
To summer winds and insects happy wings
That sport about the meadow the bright day
And see the bright beetles in the clear lake play

1841

Key Terms

Sonnet – a verse form consisting of 14 lines in iambic pentameter with rhymes
arranged according to a fixed scheme, usually divided either into an octave and
sestet or, in the Shakespearean sonnet, into three quatrains and a couplet.
Clare's sonnet uses rhyming couplets.

Reading for meaning

1 Make a list of the things that Clare likes about summer.

2 Which of the senses does this description appeal to the most? Which line does not appeal to this sense?

3 How does Clare lead us through the summer landscape as a way of organising his description?

4 Why would the insects be flying on "happy wings"?

5 Does this poem evoke a particular place, or is it simply a general description of the summer?

6 What would you say was the mood of this poem?

Literary techniques

1 How many of the lines in this poem contain some alliteration?

2 How would you describe the rhythm of this poem?

3 What is the effect of using rhyming couplets?

4 How do the alliteration, rhythm and rhyme in this poem work together to help to create its mood?

5 How does Clare use movement and stillness in the poem to give variety to the picture he creates?

6 The only simile in the poem comes in the line "Where reed clumps rustle like a wind shook wood". What else is unusual about the line? At what time of year are woods most likely to be shaken by the wind?

Themes

Clare attempts to capture a summer landscape with an almost cinematic vision. His eye moves from the sky to the lake in front of him as he notices the flowers, trees, birds and insects that reflect the summer in his part of the world. The one jarring note in his picture is the idea of the woods being shaken by the wind; a foretaste of autumn.

Introduction: preparing for the poetry questions

This section will explain how Section B of the English Literature exam works, and give you some general advice on how to approach the questions.

The questions

The questions in Section B of the English Literature exam ask you to compare modern poems and poems from the pre-1914 poetry bank. The modern poems are grouped in two groups of two poets – Seamus Heaney and Gillian Clarke in one group, and Carol Ann Duffy and Simon Armitage in the other. You should answer only one question, which means that the modern poems you will discuss in your essay will be EITHER by Seamus Heaney and Gillian Clarke OR by Carol Ann Duffy and Simon Armitage.

You are given a choice of questions to answer. All the questions ask you to focus on four poems in your answer, and give you a theme for your comparison, such as death, nature or the techniques that the poets use to create effects.

The questions ask you to compare the four poems in different ways:

- Some questions name four poems for you to compare.
- Some questions name one or two of the poems and allow you to choose the others.
- Some questions ask you to compare all four of the poems in a single essay.
- Some questions are in two parts – you compare two poems in part (a), and two others in part (b).

All the questions, however, require you to refer to both modern and pre-1914 poems in your answer.

Answering the questions

If you choose to answer a two-part question (see above), each part will ask you to compare two poems. Look again at the Exam Skills Focus on page 43 to see how to approach a simple comparison question.

Most questions ask you to compare all four poems in a single essay. This is a more complex task, as you have to have all four poems in mind as you write, rather than just two. However, your approach to a comparison essay of this type should be exactly the same as for an essay comparing two poems.

Questions that do not specify which poems to compare need to be considered carefully, as your choice of poems is very important.

- Some topics will allow you to discuss four quite similar poems.
- For some topics you might choose pairs of poems that are in sharp contrast with each other.
- For other topics you might find that your four poems cover various different aspects of the theme.

For example, imagine that you had decided to answer this question:

> **Compare the way that poets write about death in at least four poems you have studied. Write about "November" by Simon Armitage, one poem by Carol Ann Duffy and two poems from the pre-1914 poetry bank.**

The first step in preparing an answer to this question is to think about what other poems deal with the theme of death.

Death is the theme of a number of poems by Carol Ann Duffy:

- "Ann Hathaway" is about Shakespeare's widow thinking about her dead husband
- "Salome" discusses the destructiveness of casual sex
- "Education for Leisure" is told by a potential murderer.

These poems in the pre-1914 poetry bank also deal with death:

- "On My First Sonne" is about the death of a close relative
- "The Song of the Old Mother" is about the approach of death
- "The Affliction of Margaret" is told by an aged parent who fears for the life of her child
- "The Man He Killed" is about death in war
- "Tichborne's Elegy" is about a young man facing death
- "My Last Duchess" and "The Laboratory" are told from the point of view of murderers
- "Ulysses" is about old age and facing up to death.

How do you choose from such a long list? One way of narrowing down the field is to choose poems that relate to the named poem, "November", in other ways as well. Death is certainly a major theme in the poem, but it also has some interesting thing to say about ageing and the relationships between parents and children. Therefore, "Ulysses" in the pre-1914 poetry bank is a good match because it looks at old age and death, and contrasts Ulysses with his son. The theme of death is treated from the point of view of a young man in "Tichborne's Elegy", and so would provide a good contrast with "November" and "Ulysses". From the Carol Ann Duffy selection you could choose "Education for Leisure" as it would go well with "Tichborne's Elegy".

As you can see, the choice of one poem affects the way that you look at the other available choices. Your success in this part of the exam will depend to a great extent on your ability to make sensible choices.

Themes

The analysis grids on pages 180–182 will help you decide which poems can be compared effectively with which. You will see that the examiners have chosen the poems from each author quite carefully, so that you have a choice of poems and poets on a limited number of themes. This will be very important in your revision. The message this arrangement clearly gives is: **Revise according to theme.**

The table also reveals that some of the poems address more than one theme. You should revise such poems more than once, grouping them in your revision with other poems on each of the themes they cover.

Poems by Seamus Heaney and Gillian Clarke: analysis grid

Author & title	Content	Theme	Format & point of view
Seamus Heaney			
Storm on the Island	Description of a storm on a bleak island	Nature	Blank verse 1st person plural perspective
The Perch	Description of perch in the Bann river	Nature	Couplets Half rhymes 1st person perspective
Blackberry-Picking	An account of blackberry-picking – the fruit does not keep	Nature Passage of time	Couplets Half rhymes 1st person perspective Autobiographical
Death of a Naturalist	A boy suddenly experiences guilt and fear after stealing tadpoles	Nature Passage of time	Blank verse 1st person perspective Autobiographical
Digging	A son reflects on the skill of his father and his own very different skills	Character study Love/emotional ties Passage of time Parents and children	Free verse 1st person perspective Autobiographical
Mid-Term Break	A boy away at school returns home for his brother's funeral	Death Love/emotional ties Parents and children	Three-line stanzas 1st person perspective Autobiographical
Follower	A description of how old age has reversed the roles of father and son	Death Love/emotional ties Parents and children Passage of time	Quatrains Different rhyme schemes 1st person perspective Autobiographical
At a Potato Digging	A description of digging up potatoes	Death Nature Politics/History	Quatrains Different rhyme schemes 3rd person perspective
Gillian Clarke			
Catrin	A mother reflects on the relationship between herself and her daughter	Love/emotional ties Parents and children Passage of time	Free verse 1st person perspective Autobiographical
Baby-sitting	A baby-sitter worries about how the baby will feel if it wakes	Love/emotional ties Parents and children	Free verse 1st person perspective Autobiographical
Mali	A grandmother describes the birth of her granddaughter and a return to old ties	Parents and children Love/emotional ties	Seven-line stanzas 1st person perspective Autobiographical
A Difficult Birth, Easter 1998	A description of a ewe giving birth to two lambs – linked to the troubles in Ireland	Politics/History Nature	Five-line stanzas 1st and 2nd person perspective Autobiographical
The Field-mouse	An injured field-mouse, found by the speaker's child, suffers and dies	Nature Parents and children	Nine-line stanzas 1st person perspective Autobiographical
October	A description of October, a funeral and why the poet feels compelled to write	Death Passage of time Nature Love/emotional ties	Six-line stanzas 1st person perspective Autobiographical
On the Train	A woman wants to phone her lover from the train	Love/emotional ties	Six-line stanzas 1st person perspective Autobiographical
Cold Knap Lake	A child is pulled from a lake and resuscitated by the speaker's mother	Parents and children The passage of time	Free verse 1st person perspective Autobiographical

Poems by Carol Ann Duffy and Simon Armitage: analysis grid

Author & title	Content	Theme	Format & point of view
Carol Ann Duffy			
Havisham	An embittered old woman remembers a lost love now turned to hatred	Love/emotional ties Resentment Character study	Persona/1st person perspective Quatrains
Elvis's Twin Sister	Elvis Presley's twin sister lives a life of quiet contemplation in a convent	Character study	Persona/1st person perspective Five-line stanzas Some rhyme
Anne Hathaway	William Shakespeare's widow remembers her life with the great poet and playwright	Love/emotional ties Character study	Persona/1st person perspective Sonnet
Salome	The morning after her famous dance Salome wakes up with a head on her pillow	Love/emotional ties Character study	Persona/1st person perspective Irregular stanzas Some rhyme
Before You Were Mine	A girl reflects on her mother's life before her birth, based on what her mother has told her	Love/emotional ties Passage of time Parents and children	1st person perspective Autobiographical Five-line stanzas
We Remember Your Childhood Well	Parents disagree with their child over the interpretation of the child's memories	Parents and children Resentment Passage of time	Persona/1st person plural perspective Dramatic monologue Three-line stanzas
Education for Leisure	A lonely unemployed person uses killing as a means of self-assertion and pleasure	Murder/death Resentment Outsider Character study	Persona/1st person perspective Quatrains
Stealing	A thief confesses some of his crimes and explains his motivation	Outsider Character study	Persona/1st person perspective Five-line stanzas
Simon Armitage			
from *Book of Matches*: "Mother, any distance greater than a single span"	A mother helps a son to measure up his new home – the son wants and fears freedom	Parents and children Love/emotional ties	1st person perspective Autobiographical Irregular verse form
from *Book of Matches*: "My father thought it bloody queer"	A son faces his father's scorn when he returns home with a pierced ear	Parents and children Passage of time	1st person perspective Autobiographical Irregular verse form
Homecoming	A lover reflects on an argument that his partner had in her youth	Parents and children Love/emotional ties Passage of time	1st person perspective Irregular verse form
November	John takes his grandma to an old people's home and reflects on mortality	Love/emotional ties Passage of time Death	1st person perspective Dramatic monologue Irregular verse form
Kid	Robin, Batman's sidekick, has grown up, while Batman has grown old	Character study Passage of time Resentment	1st person perspective Dramatic monologue Irregular verse form
from *Book of Matches*: "Those bastards in their mansions"	A reflection on social inequality from the point of view of a rebel	Outsider Reflections on society	Persona/1st person perspective Sonnet
From *Book of Matches*: "I've made out a will"	The speaker leaves most of his body to medical science, but not his heart	Death Love	1st person perspective Sonnet
Hitcher	A tired and frustrated motorist murders a free-spirited hitch-hiker	Outsider Resentment Murder/death	Persona/1st person perspective Irregular verse form

Pre-1914 poetry bank: analysis grid

Author	Title	Content	Theme	Format & point of view
Ben Jonson	On My First Sonne	Lament for the death of the poet's son	Parents and children Love/emotional ties Death	Sonnet 1st person perspective Autobiographical
William Butler Yeats	The Song of the Old Mother	A mother compares the hard work in her life with the idleness of youth	Parents and children Love/emotional ties Passage of time	Couplets Persona/1st person perspective
William Wordsworth	The Affliction of Margaret	A mother tells of her distress – she has not heard from her only son in over seven years	Parents and children Love/emotional ties Passage of time	Seven-line stanzas Regular rhyme scheme Persona/1st person perspective
William Blake	The Little Boy Lost *and* The Little Boy Found	A boy is deserted by his father and returned to his mother by God	Parents and children Love/emotional ties	Ballad metre 3rd person perspective and direct speech
Chidiock Tichborne	Tichborne's Elegy	A man about to be executed reflects on his life	Death Passage of time	Six-line stanzas Regular rhyme scheme Autobiographical
Thomas Hardy	The Man He Killed	A soldier reflects on the fact that enemies in war might not be enemies in their ordinary life	Death Reflections on society	Quatrains ABAB rhyme scheme Direct speech
Walt Whitman	Patrolling Barnegat	A description of a storm at sea	Nature	Sonnet 14 lines all ending in -ing 3rd person perspective
William Shakespeare	Sonnet 130	A love poem which attacks the clichés usually associated with such writing	Love/emotional ties	Sonnet 1st person perspective Autobiographical
Robert Browning	My Last Duchess	A wealthy duke describes how he had his previous wife killed for being too friendly to others	Death/murder Resentment Character study	Dramatic monologue Rhyming couplets with use of enjambment Persona/1st person perspective
Robert Browning	The Laboratory	A woman consumed by jealousy of her rivals visits an apothecary's laboratory to buy poison	Death/murder Resentment Character study	Dramatic monologue Rhyming couplets Strong rhythm Persona/1st person perspective
Alfred Tennyson	Ulysses	The famous Greek hero reflects on his life and resolves to go on one last voyage	Death Passage of time Character study	Dramatic monologue Strong regular rhythm Persona/1st person perspective
Oliver Goldsmith	The Village Schoolmaster	Description of a well-respected school teacher	Character study	Rhyming couplets 3rd person perspective
Alfred Tennyson	The Eagle	A description of an eagle on a mountain	Nature	Triplets 3rd person perspective
Gerard Manley Hopkins	Inversnaid	A description of a landscape	Nature	Couplets Frequent alliteration 3rd person perspective
John Clare	Sonnet	A description of the beauties of summer	Nature	Sonnet 1st person perspective

Assessing your answers

The Assessment Objectives for this part of the exam are:

1 Respond to texts critically, sensitively and in detail, using textual evidence as

2 Explore how language, structure and forms contribute to the meaning of texts
   different approaches to texts and alternative interpretations

3 Explore relationships and comparisons within and between texts, selecting and evaluating
   relevant material.

With a partner discuss which of these objectives you find most difficult.
Share ways in which you try to cope with these requirements.

The skills that you need to show in your answer, and the content that you need to include, are
listed in the examiner's mark scheme. The mark scheme for grades A*, A and B is given on
page 193, and the scheme for grades C and D below. You will be referring to these mark
schemes later as you assess some sample essays.

Read through the mark schemes with a partner and make sure you both understand what the
examiners are looking for in your answer.

How do the mark schemes relate to the Assessment Objectives that you have just studied?

English Literature mark scheme (poetry): grades C and D

Skills		Content	
17–20 marks (notional Grade D)	• some focus on the task • awareness of feeling(s) and attitude(s) • range of comments on specific details • identification of effects intended/achieved • explained response to character/situation/ideas • specific feature(s) of language interest identified • structured comments on similarities or differences	17–24 marks	Answers are likely to include: • treatment of at least 3 poems, including pre- and post-1914 • focus on reasons/attitudes/range of task • explained/sustained response to details of feelings/attitudes/ideas • identification/explanation of writers' language and techniques • structured/sustained comparison/contrast
21–24 marks (notional Grade C)	• sustained relevant knowledge • structured response to task • appropriate comment on meaning/style • explanation of how effects are achieved • effective use of details to support answer • sustained response to situations or ideas • feature(s) of language interest explained • sustained focus on similarities/differences		

MOCK QUESTION 1

Compare the way that poets write about death in at least four poems you have studied.

Write about "November" by Simon Armitage, one poem by Carol Ann Duffy and two poems from the pre-1914 poetry bank.

Remember to compare:

◥ the deaths in the poems

◥ how the poets present death by the ways in which they write about it

◥ how the poets use language, structure and other effects to bring out what they are saying.

Planning and structuring your response

There are many poems about death that you could choose to answer this question. One good choice is "November", "Education for Leisure", "Ulysses" and "Tichborne's Elegy", as explained on page 179 above.

Your exam response will require careful planning based on the poems you have chosen and the aspects of the poems you have been asked to write about. The question asks you to cover four major areas:

- The deaths in the poems
- How the poets present death
- How the poets use language and other techniques
- How the poems are structured.

The grid below will help you to begin comparing and contrasting the poems, and to think about how to structure your essay. Copy it out and fill in the gaps.

	Deaths	Presentation	Language/techniques	Structure
November	Old woman – accepts that old age will lead to death.	Speaker talks to John, as they take his granny to a home. Afterwards they drink together. John upset but realises he will die too.	Simple descriptive language – evening imagery.	Simple narrative. Hospital, car, home. Descriptive at first – reflections at end.
Education for Leisure	Young man wants to cause death. Animals at first but people later?			
Ulysses	Older man – refuses to give up through old age.			
Tichborne's Elegy	Young man facing death – upset that life is so short.			

Share your completed grid with a partner and discuss major areas that you might be able to compare and contrast. Then share your ideas with the rest of the class.

Below is an essay plan in response to the question.

With a partner discuss how the plan has been organised. Is it adequate? What would you add to it?

With your partner or in small groups find evidence to support the statements made in the plan.

November
Modern setting
Old people and death
Granny dying but leads to thoughts of death for younger people
Granny has 'given up'
Young people take refuge in drink
Addressed to 'John'
Very simple language – play on words
Simple narrative structure

Education for Leisure
Modern setting
Young person – wants to cause death
Kills harmless animals and person?
Killing is exciting and gives status
Simple language
Simple narrative – suspense at end

DEATH

Ulysses
Set in past
Old people and death
Nobody dying yet but speaker won't give in
Old person vows further action
Invites others to join him
Dramatic monologue – addressed to sailors at end
Powerful imagery – strong rhythms
Mostly simple narrative – some flashback

Tichborne's Elegy
Set in past
Young person – regrets own death
Awaiting execution
Death as untimely end
Elaborately developed images – some biblical
No narrative – use of refrain

Analysing sample responses

Below is an extract from a 'D' response to the question. Read it through and then use the examiner's mark scheme on page 183 to identify why it gained a D. One example has been given to start you off: try to find at least two more.

1

The main thing about attitudes to death in "November", "Education for Leisure", "Ulysses" and "Tichborne's Elegy" is that two of the speakers are thinking about their own deaths ("Ulysses" and "Tichborne's Elegy") whilst two of them are concerned with the death of others. ("November" and "Education for Leisure"). Another difference is that the speaker in "Education for Leisure" is thinking about causing death. The most positive of the poems is "Ulysses" with its decision to:

strive, to seek, to find and not to yield

The most negative is "Tichborne's Elegy" which just goes on about the shortness of life. The speaker in "Education for Leisure" sees death as a way of getting power and enjoyment out of a dull life.

In "November" John takes his grandma to a home and leaves her there to die. The poem talks about how upsetting this is, but also how it has a positive effect on John and his outlook on life. The most positive poem is "Ulysses" because although the speaker realises he is coming to the end of his life, he battles on and will not give in.

In "Ulysses", the speaker knows he is old and that he should slow down "How dull it is to pause" but he still wants to get on with his life instead of letting his life pass him by and accepting death like in "November".

structured comments on similarities or differences

Below is an extract from a 'C' response to the question. Read it through and then use the examiner's mark scheme on page 183 to identify why it gained a C. One example has been given to start you off: try to find at least two more.

2

You can tell that Ulysses is not going to give up because of the way he expresses his plans:

To strive, to seek, to find and not to yield

The rhythm of this is like he is banging his fist on the table with each point. In "Tichborne's Elegy" the repetition of

And now I live and now my day is done

makes the whole poem sound mournful and makes the process of death seem sort of inevitable. The rhythm of the line is as regular as Tennyson's but it is not as strong because it doesn't repeat anything like the 'to' of "Ulysses". Instead it repeats 'and now' as if death followed on naturally from life and there is nothing we can do about it.

This same idea is expressed in "November" by the simple but effective statement about the impending death of the Grandma, "We have brought her here to die and we know it". The matter of fact statement gives the feeling of being very final. "We know it" makes death seem inevitable.

The speaker in "Ulysses" presents death in a negative way "eternal silence", "gloom" and "Death closes all" which signal the end as depressing. However, despite this, the speaker looks forward to the rest of his life in a positive way "for my purpose holds / To sail ... until I die" because he is "Strong in will / To strive ... not to yield". The reason for this positive attitude comes from the speaker's earlier active life. He is used to travelling, meeting others and accepting challenges.

appropriate comment on meaning/style

Over to you ...

Now answer the question yourself, bearing in mind what you need to do to score a Grade C. You can write about the poems already discussed or make your own choice. Remember that you have no more than 1 hour in the exam to choose a question, select your poems, plan your answer and write it.

Getting a Grade C

Compare the way that poets write about murders or possible murders in at least four poems you have studied.

Write about "Hitcher" by Simon Armitage, "Education for Leisure" by Carol Ann Duffy and two poems from the pre-1914 poetry bank.

Remember to compare:

◥ the murders in the poems

◥ how the poets present murder by the ways in which they write about it.

Planning and structuring your response

This is a very specific question and can only be answered by considering certain poems from the pre-1914 poetry bank. The two most obvious choices are "My Last Duchess" and "The Laboratory" by Robert Browning, as they are narrated by murderers.

All four poems consider murderers; two of them have already committed their crimes, while two seem to be on the point of committing them.

The grid below should help you think about what you need to focus on in the poems. Copy it out and fill in the gaps.

Hitcher	Education for Leisure	My Last Duchess	The Laboratory
Killer jealous of victim			
	Kills to make himself feel more important		
		Likes/loves victim	
			Has to get help from the chemist
Set in present day			
	Uses dramatic monologue technique		
		Regular rhyme scheme but many run-on lines	
			Light rhythm – tone not too serious

The question has two parts and you need to address both of these if you are to gain full marks. The first part asks you to focus on the content of the four poems, while the second part asks you to discuss the way the poems are written.

On page 189 there is a plan for the first part of the essay. Look at the plan with a partner and decide if there is anything that could be added.

On your own, draw a similar diagram that will cover the points that you will need to make in the second part of your essay.

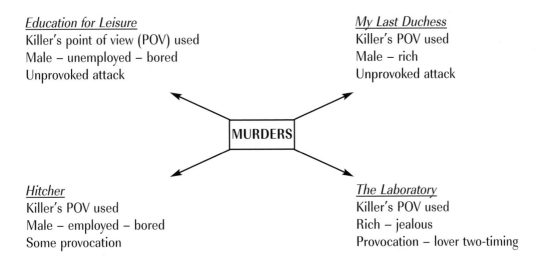

Education for Leisure
Killer's point of view (POV) used
Male – unemployed – bored
Unprovoked attack

My Last Duchess
Killer's POV used
Male – rich
Unprovoked attack

MURDERS

Hitcher
Killer's POV used
Male – employed – bored
Some provocation

The Laboratory
Killer's POV used
Rich – jealous
Provocation – lover two-timing

Analysing sample responses

Below is an extract from a 'D' response to the question. Read it through and then use the examiner's mark scheme on page 183 to identify why it gained a D. One example has been given to start you off. Then suggest ways in which this answer could be improved.

awareness of feeling(s) and attitude(s)

1

"Hitcher" by Simon Armitage, "Education for Leisure" by Carol Ann Duffy, "My Last Duchess" and "The Laboratory" by Robert Browning all deal with the theme of murder. All four of the poets have chosen to write from the point of view of the killer and in doing so they seem to want to give the reader some insight into the killer's mind. Probably the strangest murder is the one described in "My Last Duchess" as the Duke seems to have had his wife murdered simply for smiling too much. The most chilling murder is probably the one that is about to take place in "Education for Leisure". In this poem the murderer wants to kill just to make himself feel big. The murder in "Hitcher" is sort of understandable, because the speaker has got a horrible life and the Hitcher's life is free and easy – though killing somebody for this reason is hardly right! The woman in "The Laboratory" seems to have the strongest reason for wanting to kill as her lover is being unfaithful to her.

The four killers are all very different. The two poems by Browning show rich people whereas the killer in "Hitcher" is just about holding onto his job and the one in "Education for Leisure" is unemployed. In terms of why they kill, the Duke and the unemployed person seem to be the most similar. They kill or want to kill not because they hate the other person but because they want to say something about themselves. The Duke can't stand the thought of his wife not respecting his 'nine-hundred-years-old' name and the unemployed person wants everyone to realise that he is a 'genius'. At least the driver of the car is provoked by the contrast between his life and the hitcher's and he seems to be acting out of a fit of jealousy. The woman in "The Laboratory" is also motivated

Continued ▶▶▶

by jealousy of the woman who has taken her man. The main difference between these two is that the driver acts in a fit of anger whilst the woman plans her murder and goes to the poisoner for help to carry it out. Like the person in "Education for Leisure" she is quite excited by the power that killing someone gives and she even imagines killing off some of her other rivals at court.

The reader gains some understanding of the reasons for murder in all of the poems. The Duke is so powerful that he can boast about his killing to someone who has come to arrange his next marriage, and he appears to be a cold and calculating person who was too proud even to tell his wife off for her behaviour. The woman wanting to kill her rival in love is also quite easy to understand. The two modern killers are more puzzling - why does the driver react so violently and why does the unemployed person need to kill to make himself feel good? Neither Simon Armitage nor Gillian Clarke offer obvious answers to these questions and it is left up to the reader to decide.

Below is an extract from a 'C' response to the question. Read it through and then use the examiner's mark scheme on page 183 to identify why it gained a C. One example has been given to start you off. Then suggest ways in which this answer could be improved.

explanation of how effects are achieved

2

The language and style of these four poems is very different. In "My Last Duchess" Robert Browning uses rhyming couplets throughout but there are so many run on lines that you hardly notice this as you read. An example of this can be seen at the very start of the poem:

> That's my last Duchess painted on the wall,
> Looking as if she were alive. I call
> That piece a wonder, now:

In "The Laboratory" Browning also uses rhyming couplets but because most of the lines are end stopped the rhyming is much more noticeable. The use of such obvious rhyme somehow makes the poem seem less serious than "My Last Duchess". The rhythm also adds to this effect:

> Which is the poison to poison her prithee?

The "Hitcher" is much simpler than the Browning poems and hardly uses rhyme at all. The main device that Armstrong uses for emphasis is line length. After the first description of the hitcher it comes as quite a shock when you get to the line

> I let him have it

Gillian Clarke uses regular stanzas and a uniform line length in her poem and it is generally understated. This makes the final short sentence very shocking:

> I touch your arm.

Suddenly the reader realises that he or she could be the victim of such a motiveless killer.

Over to you ...

Now answer the question yourself, bearing in mind what you need to do to score a Grade C. You can write about the poems already discussed or make your own choice. Remember that you have no more than 1 hour in the exam to choose a question, select your poems, plan your answer and write it.

Getting a Grade C

As well as questions on the theme of poems, you may also be asked to look at more technical aspects such as **poetic form** or **use of imagery**. Here is a question on imagery.

> ## MOCK QUESTION 3
>
> (a) Compare the way that Seamus Heaney and Gillian Clarke use imagery by writing about "Death of a Naturalist" and "A Difficult Birth".
>
> (b) Compare the imagery used in any two poems in the pre-1914 poetry bank.
>
> Remember to compare:
>
> ◥ the words, phrases and imagery used by each poet
>
> ◥ how they present their feelings by the way in which they write about them.

Planning and structuring your response

This question is in two parts, which can be treated effectively as separate questions. The poems in question (a) have been specified; "Death of a Naturalist" uses both natural and military imagery, while "A Difficult Birth" uses natural and religious imagery. This may lead you to choose poems in your answer to question (b) which use a similar kind of imagery, although this isn't strictly necessary. William Blake's "The Little Boy Lost/The Little Boy Found" uses a combination of natural and religious imagery, while "Tichborne's Elegy" uses a variety of images, many taken from nature, to comment on his impending death.

These four poems would make a good choice as they all contain natural imagery as well as other elements.

Copy out and fill in the table below to help you think about what to focus on in your answer to this question.

	Natural imagery	Other imagery used
Death of a Naturalist		Hand grenades etc.
A Difficult Birth, Easter 1998	Birth of lamb	
The Little Boy Lost and The Little Boy Found		Personal intervention of God
Tichborne's Elegy	Crop of corn, field of tares	

Now use the table to prepare an essay plan for the question.

The main differences between a C and a D answer to this question are listed in the examiner's mark grid on page 183. Study this grid with a partner and discuss the difference in each case between:

- identification (D) and explanation (C)
- explained response (D) and sustained response (C)
- structured comments (D) and a sustained focus (C).

Analysing sample responses

Below is an extract from a 'D' response to question (a). Read it through and then use the examiner's mark scheme on page 183 to identify why it gained a D. One example has been given to start you off. Then suggest ways in which this answer could be improved.

Both of these poems use a combination of imagery to get their message across. "Death of a Naturalist" by Seamus Heaney uses natural and military imagery to convey what happened to him. Gillian Clarke uses natural and political imagery in "A Difficult Birth, Easter 1998".

It is interesting that both of the poets have used natural imagery; perhaps this is because nature doesn't change much over the years and we can all understand natural ideas like growth, birth and death. Seamus Heaney and Gillian Clarke use natural imagery because of where they live and work. Heaney grew up in the countryside and Clarke had a farm so it is perhaps obvious that they would talk about things like frogs and lambs.

The other images that these poets use are less expected and in some cases quite clever. You don't normally think of frogs as hand-grenades but in "Death of a Naturalist" when Heaney is talking about feeling frightened of the frogs the similarity in shape comes to mind as well as the threat posed by a hand grenade - or frog on this occasion. Gillian Clarke uses lots of different connections when she is talking about the birth of a lamb at Easter. She connects what is happening on her farm with what is happening in the news through the title of her poem, "A Difficult Birth" but she also connects this Easter with another political event, the Easter Rising of 1916. The idea of hope at Easter is also conveyed through her references to the rebirth of Jesus.

specific feature(s) of language interest identified

Below is an extract from a 'C' response to question (b). Read it through and then use the examiner's mark scheme on page 183 to identify why it gained a C. One example has been given to start you off.

> William Blake's use of a fen as a place of danger for a child is realistic but it also suits the purpose of his poem. Fens are dangerous places but at night often strange lights appear above them caused by marsh gas. The fen makes the reader fearful for the child and the light allows Blake to introduce an image of God. As with Gillian Clarke there is a subtle reference to the Bible in describing God as a light, as he lead the children of Israel through the desert in this form according to the book of Exodus. However, Blake is quite vague about the natural things he describes. We are simply told, for instance that 'the mire was deep'.
>
> Charles Tichborne is also vague in his use of images. He is less interested in the images themselves than in the ideas they convey. In fact if he had gone on about the wonderfulness of the feast this might have distracted the reader from his message. The reference to 'corn' and 'tares' is probably intended to remind his readers of the story in the Bible rather than real corn and weeds. Perhaps his most striking use of natural imagery is in the line 'My fruit is fallen, and yet my leaves are green'. This is a very unnatural situation and emphasises the unnaturalness of his fate.

appropriate comment on meaning/style

Over to you ...

Now answer the question yourself, bearing in mind what you need to do to score a Grade C. You can write about the poems already discussed or make your own choice. Remember that you have no more than 1 hour in the exam to choose a question, select your poems, plan your answer and write it.

English Literature mark scheme (poetry): grades A*, A and B

Skills		Content	
25–28 marks (notional Grade B)	• sustained and developed response to task • some independent exploration and insight • appreciation of writer's concerns/attitudes/ideas • details linked to writer's intentions and purposes • measured/qualified/exploratory response to writer's ideas and/or methods • features of language interest explored • developed comparison/contrast of style/ideas/form	25–36 marks	Answers are likely to include: • treatment of at least 4 poems, including 2 pre- and 2 post-1914 • exploration/development of terms/implications of task • sensitive/critical response to situation/character/meaning • developed/analytical comment on/response to writer's intended/implied purposes • evaluative comparison/contrast
29–32 marks (notional Grade A)	• sensitive insight into writer's methods, purposes and characteristics • sensitive independent exploration of context/meaning/response • analysis of writer's use of language and effect(s) on readers • insight into structure and significance of patterns of detail • evaluative comparison and contrast		
33–36 marks (notional Grade A*)	• consistent, independent insight • independent discovery and interpretation of significant details • convincing/imaginative interpretation • close textual evaluation or analysis • independent analytical/ evaluative comparison/contrast		

Getting a Grade A

Compare the ways that poets use nature in four or more of the poems you have studied, including at least one by each poet. You should write about "The Field-Mouse" by Gillian Clarke, and compare it with at least one poem by Seamus Heaney and two poems from the pre-1914 poetry bank.

Planning and structuring your response

There is no shortage of poems on nature in the work of Seamus Heaney. In fact all of his poems concern nature in some way, even "Mid-term Break", but suitable poems to compare might be:

"Blackberry-Picking", "Storm on the Island", "Perch" and "Death of a Naturalist".

In the pre-1914 poetry bank the following poems might be suitable:

"Patrolling Barnegat", "The Eagle", "Inversnaid" and Clare's "Sonnet".

One approach would be to compare descriptions of nature. "Storm on the Island", "Patrolling Barnegat" and "Sonnet" would work alongside "The Field Mouse" as it would give you two winter and two summer poems.

The question asks you to discuss how poets use nature. This means that you should think about what they describe and the lessons they draw from it.

Copy out and fill in the table below, using your own choice of poems. Then use the table to prepare an essay plan for the question.

	What is described	What lesson is drawn from description
The Field-Mouse	A field-mouse is killed during hay-making	
Storm on the Island		The harshness of existence in the countryside
Patrolling Barnegat		
Sonnet	A summer landscape	

Swap your plan with a partner's. Can you suggest any improvements to their plan, such as things they have missed out? Is there anything in their plan that you could use in yours?

Revise your own plan, if necessary, when you have listened to your partner's feedback.

Analysing sample responses

Below is an extract from a 'B' response to the question. Read it through and then use the examiner's mark scheme on page 194 to identify why it gained a B. One example has been given to start you off. Then suggest ways in which this answer could be improved.

The "field Mouse", "Storm on the Island", "Patrolling Barnegat" and "Sonnet" all include descriptions of nature and all four poems use these descriptions as a means of commenting on human life and attitudes. "Storm on the Island" and "Patrolling Barnegat" use the power of the storm to comment on the weakness and insignificance of humanity. "The field Mouse" and "Sonnet" are both set in the summer but one focuses on happiness whilst the other comments on death and war.

"Storm on the Island" is written from the point of view of an islander and at first attempts to seem unconcerned by the storm saying that 'We are prepared' and 'there are no stacks or stoops that can be lost'. But as the poem progresses the fear of the storm becomes more explicit. The absence of trees is an advantage because they will not make a disturbing noise. The sound of the sea, which is normally a comforting background noise,

spits like a tame cat
Turned savage.

Finally the speaker admits that sitting through a storm is like being in a war zone as the wind 'dives and strafes', space is 'a salvo' and the inhabitants are 'bombarded'. These military images suggest the violence of the storm as well as the powerlessness of the victims. The final line of the poem could be defiant or, with its reference to fearing a 'huge nothing,' it might be reference to people's fear of death.

"Patrolling Barnegat" also emphasises the power of the storm. Its power and energy is suggested by the fact that every line ends with a verb in the present continuous tense and sounds are suggested by a great deal of insistent alliteration. The hissing of the snow, for instance being suggested by the 's' sounds of

On beachy slush and sand spirts of snow fierce slanting

The storm with its 'demonic laughter' seems to have its own personality, but the human world is dim and indistinct

(That in the distance! is that a wreck? is the red signal flaring?)

and the human figures are described as 'struggling', 'weird' forms rather than as people as if there was no place for the patrollers in such a fierce place.

The energy of these two poems is in strong contrast to Gillian Clarke's description of a typical summer event on a farm. The hay is being cut by a tractor that looks like it is sailing on a sea as the 'waves' of hay break in front of it. A neighbour's work fills the air with a 'gift of sweetness'. However the scene is far from tranquil. 'The air hums with jets' and there is 'terrible news' on the radio and the speakers children bring an injured field-mouse to be cured. The speaker is unable to deal with the field-mouse and the haymaking produces a wave of refugees. The speaker is reminded of the refugees elsewhere in Europe and dreams of her children suffering like the field mouse in the event of civil war. Unlike the first two poems "The field-Mouse" uses nature as a contrasting background for the major concerns of the poem.

features of language
interest explored

Below is an extract from an 'A' response to the question. Read it through and then use the examiner's mark scheme on page 194 to identify why it gained a A. One example has been given to start you off.

John Clare's poem is most interested in nature itself. He tries to capture the beauty of nature by describing the things he loves or likes. There is nothing remarkable about his choices, such as sunshine, fleecy clouds or quiet Moor Hens but as the poem progresses the reader builds up a picture of a tranquil English country scene. The poem is full of enthusiasm and quiet joy: the sun is 'beaming'; the flowers stain their surroundings with 'gold'; the lake is 'clear'; the insects fly on 'happy' wings and both the day and the beetles are 'bright'. The portrait also includes movement so that clouds are 'sailing to the north'; the Moor Hen 'pushes and seeks'; the 'reed clumps rustle' alliteratively in the wind; the willow leans over its lake; the heads of the hay grass 'swing to the summer winds' and the beetles 'play' in the lake. All of this detail is contained in the fourteen lines of the sonnet.

Walt Whitman's sonnet "Patrolling Barnegat" also seems mostly interested in nature itself, but unlike Clare's poem this is nature at its most powerful and violent. Rather than the traditional rhyme scheme of a sonnet Whitman ends every line with a verb, emphasising the ceaseless activity of the storm. The poem begins as it means to go on with the use of the word 'wild' twice and Whitman also uses a number of alliterative effects for emphasis or to suggest the sounds of the storm.

'Shouts of demoniac laughter, fitfully piercing and pealing' for instance gives some idea of the power of and strength of the sounds, whereas the description of the waves' 'combs careering' suggest the speed and harshness of their movement - Whitman also repeats this description to show that the waves continually move. Amongst all of this energy of 'waves, air and midnight' the human figures are 'dim weird forms' that struggle through the night 'warily watching' the storm.

analysis of writer's use of language

Over to you ...

Continue the second extract, discussing "The Field-Mouse" and "Storm on the Island" in similar way.

Getting a Grade A

MOCK QUESTION 5

Some of the poems in these selections might be considered to be depressing.

(a) Compare "Tichborne's Elegy" with one other pre-1914 poem.

(a) Compare Gillian Clarke's "October" with one poem by Seamus Heaney.

Write about:

❧ why readers might find these poems depressing

❧ how the poets write in ways that make the poems seem depressing

❧ the similarities and differences between the poems

❧ how you respond to the poems.

Planning and structuring your response

This question is in two parts, which can be treated effectively as separate questions.

The theme of "Tichborne's Elegy" is death, and there are plenty of poems with this depressing theme in the anthology. "On My First Sonne" also deals with untimely death (though this time it is the poet's son who has died, rather than the poet himself who is about to die), so you might think that these two make a good pair for comparison.

With a partner, identify the theme of "October" by Gillian Clarke. Then choose a poem by Seamus Heaney that deals with a similar theme.

The question provides bullet points that ask you to discuss why the poems might be considered depressing and how the poets write in ways that make the poems seem depressing. You can compare and contrast them (as mentioned in the third bullet point) in a table to help you focus your thoughts.

Copy out and fill in the table below, using your own choice of poems.

Poem	What is described	How it is described – techniques
Tichborne's Elegy	impending death of the poet	
On My First Sonne		simple rhythm plain choice of words simple and direct imagery
Mid-Term Break	death of the poet's brother	
October		

Now use the table to prepare an essay plan for the question.

The main differences between a B and an A grade answer to this question are listed in the examiner's mark grid on page 194. Study this grid with a partner and discuss the difference in each case between:

- some independent exploration and insight (B) and sensitive independent exploration (A)
- measured/qualified/exploratory response to writer's ideas and/or methods (B) and sensitive insight into writer's methods, purposes and characteristics (A)
- developed comparison/contrast (B) and evaluative comparison and contrast (A).

Be prepared to report your conclusions back to the class.

Analysing sample responses

Below is an extract from a 'B' response to question (a). Read it through and then use the examiner's mark scheme on page 194 to identify why it gained a B. One example has been given to start you off. Then suggest ways in which this answer could be improved.

"Tichborne's Elegy" and "On My First Sonne", both deal with the subject of death and therefore might be considered depressing by all but the most morbid of readers. "Tichborne's Elegy" is unusual in that it is a meditation on the immanent death of the poet; "On My First Sonne" is a reflection on the death of the poet's first-born child. Both poets respond deeply to these depressing events and in doing so they say things that are not necessarily depressing to the reader.

"Tichborne's Elegy" is almost certainly the more negative of the two poems. This is not surprising as very few people are likely to feel cheerful when they know they are shortly to be executed, but Tichborne makes his Elegy even more depressing by using a mournful refrain at the end of each stanza:

And now I live and now my life is done.

In the first part of the poem, Tichborne treats his life like a calculation and carefully cancels out all its positives with negatives:

My prime of youth is but a frost of cares,
My feast of joy is but a dish of pain

As well as this 'zero sum' Tichborne introduces images that speak of loss or lack of completion in terms of sunless days, unheard tales or fruit fallen before its time. Eventually the effect becomes overwhelming and you are either moved to pity Tichborne or inclined to tell him to stop complaining. What is surprising in this poem by a Christian martyr is that Tichborne does not look beyond death to his heavenly reward.

appreciation of writer's concerns/attitudes/ideas

Continued ▹ ▹ ▹

It is difficult to imagine a more depressing subject than a parent thinking about the death of his child but Ben Jonson's poem "On My First Sonne" is actually much more positive than "Tichborne's Elegy". This is partly because Jonson does take some comfort from his Christian faith and imagines his son as having escaped from the

worlds and the fleshes rage,
And if no other misery yet age

The other factor that prevents the poem from being depressing is the genuine love and tenderness that Jonson expresses in the simple dignified language of the poem. The son of his 'right hand' is something precious that has been 'lent' to him and that he has been forced to pay back, and the poet and playwright sees the boy as

his best piece of poetrie.

Jonson is of course sad at the death of his son but he blames himself for loving the boy too well. Not growing too fond of small children was a sensible precaution in the seventeenth century when infant mortality rates were very high but Jonson's final resolution not to love so strongly again leaves the reader feeling saddened on the poet's behalf.

Below is an extract from an 'A' response to question (b). Read it through and then use the examiner's mark scheme on page 194 to identify why it gained an A. One example has been given to start you off.

"Mid-term Break" and "October" could both be described as depressing poems, as they deal with death in some way and they both communicate a sense of sadness and regret. Most readers would find these topics depressing and it is therefore interesting to ask why anyone would bother to read them.

"Mid-term Break" describes a sad event in the life of the speaker. The title of the poem is therefore a little misleading as most people look forward to half terms. In Heaney's poem however the 'break' is caused by the death of his four year old brother. The poem describes the speaker's journey from school to his brother's bedside and describes the effect of the death on members of the family, neighbours and friends. The only cheerful voice in the poem is that of the baby who is too young to understand, everyone else is devastated by the event. I think that the reason people read this poem is that we are all interested in other people's lives and how they cope with tragedy is particularly revealing. Heaney describes the scene in simple and accessible language which does not force his emotions on the reader:

> The baby cooed and laughed and rocked the pram
> When I came in, and I was embarrassed
> By old men standing up to shake my hand
> And tell me they were "sorry for my trouble".

"October" also deals with a death but because the dead person is probably quite old it is less shocking than the death of the four-year old. The poem uses the time of year, October, to represent the time of life of the dead friend. October is quite late in the year and the life and growth of spring and summer have definitely gone. It tends to rain more and the things we see around us are affected by the gloomy weather. This is the case of the statue of the lion and of the plants that are described. The speaker is also quite old, it seems, and her response to the death is to write and keep death at bay. Possibly she wants to achieve a kind of Indian Summer. Gillian Clarke uses natural imagery to comment on a natural event. In a way the final stanza is quite brave as the speaker refuses to be put off by death and uses it as a spur for her creativity. This is probably what makes the poem worth reading as it examines how one person copes with a problem that faces us all.

analysis of writer's use of language and effect(s) on readers

Over to you ...

Now answer the question yourself, bearing in mind what you need to do to score a Grade A. Make your own choice of poems. Remember that you have no more than 1 hour in the exam to choose a question, select your poems, plan your answer and write it.

Getting a Grade A

The following question focuses on poetic technique rather than theme.

> ### Mock Question 6
>
> Compare how poets use dramatic monologues to shape their meaning in at least four of the poems you have studied. Write about "Education for Leisure" by Carol Ann Duffy, "Hitcher" by Simon Armitage, and two poems from the pre-1914 poetry bank.

Planning and structuring your response

There are several dramatic monologues in the pre-1914 poetry bank, but it would be wise to choose poems whose themes reflect those of the specified poems, "Education for Leisure" and "Hitcher". The two obvious candidates are "My Last Duchess" and "The Laboratory" by Robert Browning.

Dramatic monologues have some or all of the following features:

- A persona – the poem is written as if in the first person but by someone who is clearly not the poet.
- An implied listener – sometimes the listener is identified, sometimes it is simply the reader.
- Some insight into the psychology and motivation of the speaker.
- They are usually written in the present tense.

Copy out and fill in the table below, so that you can focus your thoughts on how to answer the question.

	Hitcher	Education for Leisure	My Last Duchess	The Laboratory
Persona	car driver			
Implied listener		reader		
Psychological insights			arrogant, e.g. ...	
Tense				present tense

The key words in the question are "shape meaning". With a partner discuss what you think this phrase means. Be prepared to share your ideas with the rest of the class.

Below is a student's plan for an essay answering this question. Look at the plan with a partner and decide if it could be improved.

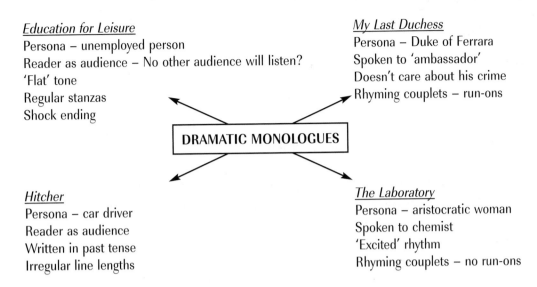

Education for Leisure
Persona – unemployed person
Reader as audience – No other audience will listen?
'Flat' tone
Regular stanzas
Shock ending

My Last Duchess
Persona – Duke of Ferrara
Spoken to 'ambassador'
Doesn't care about his crime
Rhyming couplets – run-ons

DRAMATIC MONOLOGUES

Hitcher
Persona – car driver
Reader as audience
Written in past tense
Irregular line lengths

The Laboratory
Persona – aristocratic woman
Spoken to chemist
'Excited' rhythm
Rhyming couplets – no run-ons

Analysing sample responses

Below is an extract from a 'B' response to the question. Read it through and then use the examiner's mark scheme on page 194 to identify why it gained a B. One example has been given to start you off. Then suggest ways in which this answer could be improved.

"Education for Leisure" by Carol Ann Duffy, "Hitcher" by Simon Armitage, "My Last Duchess" and "The Laboratory" by Robert Browning all use dramatic monologues techniques. Each poet has adopted the persona of an actual or potential killer in order to explore the psychology of murder.

The two poems by Robert Browning make full use of the possibilities offered by the dramatic monologue. In "My Last Duchess" Browning impersonates a Duke who is so far beyond ordinary limits that he is able to boast about the killing of his previous wife to someone who has come to arrange his next marriage. The colossal arrogance of the Duke is matched only by his desire to possess - he seems happy now that he is the one who controls access to his wife's smiles; she has become a work of art that he can show off with his other possessions. In "The Laboratory" Browning attempts to enter the mind of a woman who has been betrayed by her lover. In contrast with the rather sombre tone of "My Last Duchess" there is an air of excitement about "The Laboratory" as the woman explores the strange workplace of the poisoner and contemplates the power that the ability to kill provides. Unlike the Duke the woman wishes to take pleasure in her enemies suffering as she dies.

　　Not that I bid you spare her the pain;
　　Let death be felt and the proof remain:

The speaker in "Education for Leisure" seems to be the very opposite of excited. The poem uses very ordinary and drab language

details linked to writer's intentions and purposes

Continued ◥◥◥

and even manages to make the Bible and Shakespeare sound dull. Only when the speaker contemplates killing does the imagery become lively

I get our bread-knife and go out.

The pavements glitter suddenly.

The final line of the poem also reveals that the implied listener is much closer than we might have thought at first:

I touch your arm.

Simon Armitage's "Hitcher" has some of the features of a dramatic monologue but not all of them. Unlike the other poems it is in the past tense and describes a longer time period than that taken by the poem itself. There is no listener present in the poem and it could be just an anecdote told at any time after the event. However, Armitage does make good use of the persona and describes the central event of the poem in a dramatic way:

I let him have it

As with the other poems we get some insight into the motivation behind the driver's crime, provided by the account of his morning before he met the hitcher:

I'd been tired, under

the weather, but the ansaphone kept screaming:

One more sick-note, mister, and you're finished. Fired.

Below is an extract from an 'A' response to the question. Read it through and then use the examiner's mark scheme on page 194 to identify why it gained an A. One example has been given to start you off.

The way that the three poets shape meaning through their use of dramatic monologues varies considerably. In "My Last Duchess" Browning uses the Duke's showing off of the portrait to take his audience back through his crimes. In "The Laboratory" the woman looks back at the cause of her grievance and looks forward to carrying out her revenge. "Education for Leisure" begins with a statement of future intent:

Today I am going to kill something

and ends in a frightening present:

I touch your arm.

Only "Hitcher" is completely in the past tense and has to create a sense of shock by the way in which the events are revealed.

The personas that the poets adopt all have one thing in common but their motivations vary considerably. The driver in "The Hitcher" is probably the least complex of the four. His life is not going well and he is irritated by the contrast between his life and that of his passenger. It is interesting that the way the passenger talks is full of clichés like 'the good earth' and 'blowin' in the wind'.

He was following the sun to west from east
with just a toothbrush and the good earth for a bed. The truth,
he said, was blowin' in the wind,
or round the next bend.

This laziness of language implies a laziness of thought and suggests that the hitcher is simply avoiding the life of hard work that the driver has to face. We can thus sympathise with the driver's rage when it erupts.

We can also sympathise with the woman in "The Laboratory" as her lover is clearly treating her badly:

He is with her and they know that I know
Where they are, what they do: they believe my tears flow.

It is even possible to understand her desire to see her rival suffer in death, given the amount of suffering she has had to endure in life. We also see, in the section dealing with the speaker's desire to kill off her rivals, how dependent women of this time and social class were on male estimations of their physical beauty:

and Elise, with her head
And her breast, and her arms and her hands, should drop dead!

It is less difficult to sympathise with the Duke. Not only has he had his wife killed for a seemingly trivial reason - the fact that she smiled too easily - but he also has the arrogance to boast about it to the ambassador from his next wife. His account could be a warning but the fact that he moves quickly onto a discussion of a statue he owns suggests that he is merely arrogant. For the modern reader the Duke is mainly interesting as a study in power as he seems to be completely beyond either remorse, shame or any punishment for his actions.

The least sympathetic of the personas adopted in these four poems is that of the unemployed person in "Education for Leisure". The character seems completely cold and without remorse. He kills for pleasure and to make himself feel good. The only insight that could influence the reader's judgement is contained in the title of the poem. Perhaps with a better and more relevant educational system people would be either better able to get jobs or better able to cope with unemployment.

sensitive independent exploration
of context/meaning/response

Over to you ...

Now answer the question yourself, bearing in mind what you need to do to score a Grade A. You can write about the poems already discussed or make your own choice. Remember that you have no more than 1 hour in the exam to choose a question, select your poems, plan your answer and write it.

Acknowledgements

The publishers gratefully acknowledge the following for permission to reproduce copyright material. Whilst every effort to trace the copyright holders has been made, this has not proved possible in every case.

Text: p4 "Limbo" by Kamau Brathwaite was originally published in *The Arrivants: A New World Trilogy*, Oxford University Press, 1973; p8 "Nothing's Changed" by Tatumkhulu Afrika; p11 Curtis Brown Ltd, London, on behalf of Grace Nichols for "Island Man" from *The Fat Black Woman Poems* © Grace Nichols; p14 Bloodaxe Books for "Blessing" by Imtiaz Dharker, from *Postcards from God*, Bloodaxe Books, 1997; p17 "Two Scavengers in a Truck, Two Beautiful People in a Mercedes" by Lawrence Ferlinghetti, from *These Are My Rivers,* copyright© 1979 by Lawrence Ferlinghetti. Reprinted by permission of New Directions Publishing Corp; p21 "Night of the Scorpion" from *Poverty Poems* by Nissim Ezekiel is reproduced by permission of Oxford University Press, New Delhi; p25 David Bolt Associates for "Vultures" by Chinua Achebe from *Beware Soul Brother* published by Heninemann Educational; p28 Pollinger Limited and the New Directions Publishing Corporation for "What Were They Like?" by Denise Levertov from *Selected Poems* published by Bloodaxe Books; p48 extract from "Search For My Tongue" from *Brunizem* by Sujata Bhatt is reproduced with permission of Carcanet Press; p51 extract from "Unrelated Incidents" from *Intimate Voices: Selected Works 1965–1983* is reproduced with the permission of Tom Leonard, published by Vintage in 1995 © Tom Leonard; p55 "Half-Caste" is reproduced by kind permission of John Agard c/o Caroline Sheldon Literary Agency from *Get Back Pimple* published by Puffin in 1996; p58 "Love After Love" from *Selected Poems* by Derek Walcott is reproduced by permission of Faber and Faber Ltd; p60 "This Room" by Imtiaz Dharker from *I Speak for the Devil*, Bloodaxe Books, 2001, is reproduced with permission of Bloodaxe Books; p62 "Not My Business" by Niyi Osundare from *Songs of the Seasons*, first published by Heinemann Educational, Nigeria, 1990 is reproduced by permission of Niyi Osundare; p64 "Presents from My Aunts in Pakistan" from *Carrying My Wife* by Moniza Alvi, Bloodaxe Books, 2000, is reproduced with permission of Bloodaxe Books; p68 "Hurricane Hits England" from *Sunrise* by Grace Nichols is reproduced with permission of Curtis Brown Ltd, copyright © Grace Nichols; pp85–100 Seamus Heaney: "Storm on the Island" and "Follower" from *Death of Naturalist* (1966), "Mid-Term Break", "Death of a Naturalist", "Digging", "At a Potato Digging" and "Blackberry-Picking" from *New Selected Poems 1966–1987* (1990) and "Perch" from *Electric Light* (2001), all reprinted by permission of the publishers, Faber & Faber Ltd; pp101–15 Gillian Clarke: "October", "Baby-sitting", "Mali", "Cold Knap Lake" and "Catrin" from *Collected Poems* (1997), "A Difficult Birth" and "The Field-Mouse" from *Fivefields* (1998), all reprinted by permission of the publishers, Carcanet Press Ltd, "On the Train" reprinted by permission of the author; pp116–31 Carol Ann Duffy: "Education for Leisure" from *Standing Female Nude* (1985), "Stealing" from *Selling Manhatten* (1987), "Havisham" and "Before You Were Mine" from *The Other Country* (1998), all reprinted by permission of the publisher, Anvil Press Poetry Ltd, "Elvis's Twin Sister", "Anne Hathaway" and "Salome" from *The World's Wife* (Picador Macmillan, 1999), copyright © Carol Ann Duffy 1999, reprinted by permission of Macmillan, London, UK; pp132–47 Simon Armitage: "Hitcher", "Those bastards in their mansions" and "My father thought it bloody queer" from *Book of Matches* (1993), "Mother", "November", "Kid", "I've made out a will" and "Homecoming" from *Selected Poems* (2001), all reprinted by permission of the publishers, Faber & Faber Ltd; p150 "The Song of the Old Mother" by W B Yeats from *The Collected Poems* edited by Daniel Albright (J M Dent, 1994), reprinted by permission of A P Watt Ltd on behalf of Michael B Yeats.

Photos: Magnum Photos p5, 28 (bottom), 62; Mary Evans Photo Library p6, 99; Carlos Reyes/Andes Press Agency p8, 60; Stone p11 (bottom), 17 (bottom), 93, 95, 106, 110, 160 (bottom), 174 (bottom), 176 (bottom); Taxi p11 (middle), 25 (bottom), 91, 130; Still Pictures p14 (bottom); Imagebank p8, 23, 101 (bottom), 104, 112; Photofusion p21, 31; PA Photos p25 (top), 51, 68; Illustration Works p85 (bottom); Science Photo Library p87; Foodpix p89; Hulton Archive p 97, 124, 126, 150 (both), 152 (top), 154 (top), 158 (both), 160 (top), 162 (top), 164 (top), 166 (both), 168 (top), 170, 172 (top), 174 (top), 176 (top); OSF p108; Photolibrary Wales p114; Ronald Grant Archive p116, 140; Redferns Picture Library p118; Shakespeare Birthplace Trust p120; Eyewire p128; New Directions Publishing Corp p4, 17 (top), 28 (top); I-Afrika photos p8; Sheila Geraghty p11 (top), 68 (top); Bloodaxe Books p14 (top), 60 (top), 64; Carcanet Press p48, 101 (top); Sonya Leonard p51; The Poetry Library p55; Nigel Parry p58; Niyi Osundare p62; Caroline Forbes p85 (top); Sue Adler p116 (top); Jason Bell p132 (top); Corbis p132 (bottom), 142, 144; Royalty Free/CORBIS p134; Bridgeman Art Library p154 (bottom), 155, 156, 160 (bottom), 162 (bottom), 166 (bottom).